FILM INDIA
THE NEW GENERATION
1960-1980

An examination of India's New Cinema, its
preoccupation with a changing society and the
status of women, highlighted in the work of
19 representative directors.

THE DIRECTORATE OF FILM FESTIVALS
NEW DELHI

Editor
Uma da Cunha

Assistant Editor
Maithili Rao

With assistance from
Nirmal Goswami
Amitabha Mukherjee
Nomita Kundandas

Cover design
Zahid Sardar

Page design/layout
Dhun Dudhmul

Production
Nomita Kundandas

First published 1981

Published by the Directorate of Film Festivals,
Ministry of Information and Broadcasting,
Lok Nayak Bhavan, 4th Floor,
Khan Market, New Delhi 110 003.
Printed at Tata Press Limited, Bombay.

CONTENTS

5 FOREWORD

6 THE SETTING

8 THE CANVAS

10 It Was Time for the New Cinema
18 The Film Framework: Government Support
24 The Greatest Show-biz on Earth
30 The Indian Ethos
35 The Long and Short of It

40 THE DIRECTORS, THEIR FILMS

42 G. ARAVINDAN
46 Kanchana Sita (Golden Sita) *Malayalam*

50 SHYAM BENEGAL
54 Manthan (The Churning) *Hindi*
56 Bhumika (The Role) *Hindi*

60 BASU CHATTERJI
63 Sara Akash (The Whole Sky) *Hindi*

68 RABINDRA DHARMARAJ
72 Chakra (The Vicious Circle) *Hindi*

74 RITWIK GHATAK
78 Ajantrik (The Mechanical Man) *Bengali*

82 ADOOR GOPALAKRISHNAN
86 Kodiyettam (Ascent) *Malayalam*

90 GIRISH KARNAD
94 Kaadu (The Forest) *Kannada*
96 Ondanondu Kaladalli (Once Upon a Time) *Kannada*

100 GIRISH KASARAVALLI
103 Ghatashraddha (The Ritual) *Kannada*

106 AWTAR KAUL
109 27 Down *Hindi*

112 MANI KAUL
115 Uski Roti (A Day's Bread) *Hindi*

118 KETAN MEHTA
121 Bhavni Bhavai (A Folk Tale) *Gujarati*

3

124 SAEED MIRZA
127 Albert Pinto Ko Gussa Kyon Aata Hai
(What Makes Alberto Pinto Angry) *Hindi*

130 GOVIND NIHALANI
133 Aakrosh (Cry of the Wounded) *Hindi*

136 RAMDAS PHUTANE
139 Sarvasakshi (The Omniscient) *Marathi*

142 PATTABHI RAMA REDDY
146 Samskara (Funeral Rites) *Kannada*

148 M. S. SATHYU
152 Garm Hava (Hot Winds) *Hindi*

156 MRINAL SEN
160 Bhuvan Shome *Hindi*
162 Aakaler Sandhaney (In Search of Famine) *Bengali*

168 KUMAR SHAHANI
172 Maya Darpan *Hindi*

176 SURINDER SURI
179 Rikki Tikki Tavi (The Brave Mongoose) *English/Russian*

182 BANSI CHANDRAGUPTA
Art Director *(May 22, 1924 — June 27, 1981)*

183 NOTES ON CONTRIBUTORS

FOREWORD

What really distinguishes the New Indian Cinema is a definitive set of liberal-humanitarian values, embracing progressive solutions to urgent problems, a sensitivity to the plight of the poor and oppressed, a faith in the ultimate movement of man towards change. Drawing its inspiration largely from the neo-realists, it is a cinema of social significance and artistic sincerity, presenting a modern, humanist perspective, more durable than the fantasy world of the popular film.

The emergence of the New Indian Cinema in the late sixties as a recognisable movement was partly a reaction to the popular cinema's "other-worldliness." But perhaps the main forces behind it were the democratic and developmental processes set off after India's independence. These evoked a new awareness and led to an exploration of the seemingly imperceptible changes in a traditional society under the impact of modernising influences. This resulted in a re-examination, however tentative, of an entire value system.

A continuous, deepening exploration of life in India's changing context has been the main concern of the New Cinema. Its preoccupation is with the growing contradictions of a society in which large sections of the people, long used to passive acceptance, have meanwhile become politicised.

The New Cinema is "regional" in the sense that it speaks in terms of a recognisable situation, gives its characters a social identity and deals with situations close to life. In production too it follows a pattern different from the popular cinema: the films have low budgets, are shot on location, experiment with new actors and in many cases are based on Indian literature. Significantly, the New Cinema owes a great deal to State patronage in the form of easy loans, tax concessions, recognition through awards and a sustained effort to promote it at home and abroad.

This book, it is hoped, will provide the background for understanding recent trends. The articles cover both sides of Indian cinema's split personality and the ethos from which it emerges. There is a review of the short film movement and an outline of State assistance. For each film included in the section there are the director's profile, a detailed synopsis and stills.

The book includes a map of India, detailing the cinematic setting for easy reference.

Raghunath Raina
Director,
Directorate of Film Festivals,
New Delhi,
May 15, 1981.

5

THE SETTING

Number of States: 22 + 9 Union Territories

Number of official languages: 16, each with its own script and a considerable body of literature.

Dialects: 1652

States
1. Andhra Pradesh
2. Assam
3. Bihar
4. Gujarat
5. Haryana
6. Himachal Pradesh
7. Jammu & Kashmir
8. Karnataka
9. Kerala
10. Madhya Pradesh
11. Maharashtra
12. Manipur
13. Meghalaya
14. Nagaland
15. Orissa
16. Punjab
17. Rajasthan
18. Sikkim
19. Tamil Nadu
20. Tripura
21. Uttar Pradesh
22. West Bengal

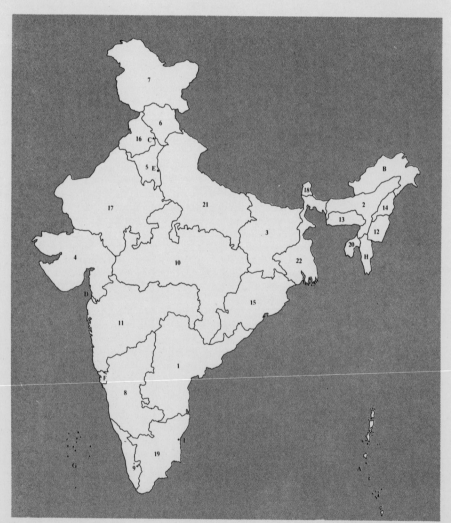

Union Territories (Federally administered)

A. Andaman/Nicobar Isles
B. Arunachal Pradesh
C. Chandigarh city
D. Dadra & Nagar Havelli
E. Delhi
F. Goa-Daman-Diu
G. Lakshadweep Island
H. Mizoram
I. Pondicherry city

Languages (against their main State)

1. Hindi: the most widely understood language
2. English: a link language
3. Sanskrit: an ancient classical language
4. Sindhi: spoken by former residents of Sind
5. Urdu: mostly in North India and pockets of the South and Bombay
6. Marathi: Maharashtra
7. Bengali: West Bengal
8. Telugu: Andhra Pradesh
9. Tamil: Tamil Nadu
10. Gujarati: Gujarat
11. Oriya: Orissa
12. Malayalam: Kerala
13. Assamese: Assam
14. Punjabi: Punjab
15. Kashmiri: Kashmir
16. Kannada: Karnataka

Population: 684 million
Cinema audience: 65 million per week
No. of films made in 1980: 742 (85% in colour)
Number of permanent cinemas: 6,368
Number of touring cinemas: 4,024
Total: roughly 10,500
Deduction: roughly 7 cinema seats to 1000 persons, one of the lowest averages, even for Asian countries. The theatres are not uniformly spread either. Touring theatres, which are peculiar to India, operate only part of the year and mostly in rural areas. Permanent cinemas usually run 3 to 4 fixed time screenings per day. Every cinema must compulsorily screen one newsreel and/or documentary each week approved by the Film Advisory Board, a government body, for which the cinema pays a rental.
Box office collection 1980/81: Rs. 3,350,000,000 (an increase of 22% over the previous year)
Levies on film collected by State Government in 1980/81: Rs. 585,000,000 (average 70% of box office)
Export earnings from films: Rs. 150,000,000 (25% increase on previous year)
Average budget of a Hindi film: Rs. 6,000,000
Average budget of multi-star film: Rs. 30,000,000
Average low-budget film: Rs. 1,500,000

Currency conversion rates in Indian denominations:
Reserve Bank of India rates
as of July 22, 1981
Rs 1 lakh (Rs. 100,000) = $11,363
Rs 1 crore (Rs. 10,000,000) = $1,136,000

THE CANVAS

India has been making films for as long as almost any other country. Today it produces the largest number of films in the world. The majority of the films are long-drawn melodramas spiced with song and dance.

The past two decades have seen the emergence of new directors with a personal vision. They have a tradition, though. Their forebears were the socially-purposeful studio film makers of the thirties and forties—a period charged with nationalistic fervour. Their concern carried over into the fifties in the realistic films of Bimal Roy, K. A. Abbas, Guru Dutt and the early Raj Kapoor.

The present polarisation between the perennial "commercial" cinema and the new "other" cinema is due mainly to the studio monopoly giving way to independent producers. The added freedom of choice strengthened the star system, making film production a highly speculative business. And so, a vacuum was created for the New Cinema, which from the start opposed all popular dictates...escapism, stars, the mass audience and an autocratic distribution system.

The five articles that follow attempt to convey the impetus and character of the contemporary Indian film scene. They constitute an enquiry into its newness and an appreciation of its scope and intentions. A distinction is made between the commercial cinema and the New Indian Cinema, which seeks to derive its artistic validity from commitment to beliefs and ideologies.

A protest meet: still from Saeed Mirza's **Albert Pinto ko Gussa Kyon Aata Hai** *(What Makes Albert Pinto Angry).*

IT WAS TIME FOR THE NEW CINEMA

An acute awareness of social problems combined with
an active protest against the establishment's way of making
popular films characterises the new film makers. To
outsiders, the protest may at times seem understated or
muted. The tone could well be the result of a society
attuned to subdued speaking. The guidelines on film censorship, with a duty to protect the many susceptibilities of a
multi-religious and secular society could perhaps moderate
the extremist's comment. To many Indians, the authentic
dissent is the voice of conscience. Its New Cinema reflects
the country's democracy on the one hand and its constraints
on the other.

Iqbal Masud analyses the genesis, growth and trends
of the New Cinema.

Film director, scriptwriter and actor (1925-1965) who brought a genuine sensitivity and pathos to Hindi cinema.: Guru Dutt

Bimal Roy (1909-1966) striking out a new trail in cinema for generations to follow.

"The metaphor of the 'New Wave' was surprisingly apt; the wave had been building up for a long time before it burst on cinematic shores." That remark of James Monaco on the French 'New Wave' (OUP, New York, 1979 p. 11) applies equally to the Indian New Wave which burst on *our* cinematic shores in the sixties.

Such new waves are the result of the mutual reinforcement of a variety of wavelets — technological changes, thematic changes, changes in theoretical approach, changes in material environment, *et al.* In a brief survey such as this I shall concentrate on the last three elements.

Silent cinema in India commenced in 1896, talkies in 1930. During the last seven decades the number of films and the power of the cinema over the masses as the main form of entertainment increased astonishingly. From a meagre 27 in 1931 the production of sound films increased to 318 in 1960. During this period the established studios/producers declined, the fly-by-night producer class, out for a fast buck, began its ascent. The character of the audience too changed. The urban middle class audiences of the twenties and thirties were swamped by the uprooted industrial workers and labourers swarming to the cities.

And yet the major theme of the Indian cinema remained within remarkably narrow parameters. There were the ever popular religious mythological films (their steady following remains loyal to this day). Very close to them were the so-called "historical" films which were equally popular exercises in myth making — glorifying some flattering chapters of Indian history. The forties and fifties saw the rise of social-reformist films — cautious critiques of obvious social evils such as the dowry system prostitution, polygamy, etc.

The end of the fifties marked the exhaustion of invention and imagination in this narrow field. A few film makers had already struck out new trails. Bimal Roy in *Do Bigha Zamin* (Two Acres of Land, 1953) took up the stark theme of a peasant driven out of land by industrialisation, ending up as a rickshaw-puller on Calcutta's streets. Satyajit Ray's *Pather Panchali* (The Song of the Road, 1955) delineated the increasing misery of a poor family in a village, focusing on a pair of children. The fact that these films were seen by large numbers, discussed and talked about, signalled the end of the monopoly of the Devotional-Historical-Social Syndrome.

The theoretical approach to film making also changed. The obvious contributory factors were the International Film Festivals (held in 1952, 1961, followed by others at shorter intervals) organised by the Directorate of Film Festivals; the founding of the Film Institute of India with courses on directing and other areas of film making; and of the National Film Archive of India (1964) which began to play a role similar to that of France's Cinematheque under Henri Langlois. The impact of the world's classics — particularly French and Japanese and of Ray's

Still from Devdas *(1955), a Bimal Roy classic.*

early films — on film makers who would later dominate the New Cinema cannot be overestimated.

I think what Kolker ('A Cinema of Loneliness', OUP, 1980 p.8) says of French cinema of the fifties and sixties sums up the attitude of Indian auteurs growing up in the sixties and seventies. They did not consider "film a substandard form of entertainment but rather a form of expression to be taken seriously — they celebrated, and analysed film as a special narrative form with a voice, a text and an audience deeply interrelated."

The changes in social and political environment were another impelling factor. The *Pax Nehruviana* (if one may so call it) — the fairly stable holding-together structure in a sub-continent with a maze of religions and a babble of tongues — which had prevailed since 1947 was drawing to a close. Industrial growth had been fair but population increase was negating the gains. Land feudalism had not been liquidated and the income gap was widening. The Chinese invasion in 1962 was a massive jolt to the national ego. Suddenly it seemed the centre could not hold, the old certainties had gone. It was time for films "to begin an ideological debate with the cultures that bred them." It was time for the New Cinema.

Satyajit Ray seen talking to the noted Indian kathak exponent, Birju Maharaj, who choreographed the dances in his film Shatranj ke Khilari *(The Chess Players). With the two masters are (left to right) art director Bansi Chandragupta, producer Suresh Jindal, and Ray's cameraman, Soumendu Roy.*

It may be illuminating to compare the French, the American and the Indian New Waves. The French New Wave was mainly the result of the devotion of a few intellectual-artists to the "personal style." The American New Wave (late sixties) operated firmly within the tradition of the Hollywood film. The Indian New Wave is in a sense unique among the mid-century world "new cinema." It can be seen on the surface as an avid response to Nouvelle Vague. At a deeper level it was propelled by the inner logic of this Indian situation. It is therefore necessary to see this New Cinema not in terms of technology or even of style but in the broadest context of social change.

Satyajit Ray, Mrinal Sen, Ritwik Ghatak were the founding fathers. Ray had a special vision of the Indian reality — hard, implacable, piercing to the heart of the matter in an unbearably truthful yet moving fashion. Mrinal is the ebullient one—experimenting with neo-realism, as well as Nouvelle Vague, and fantasy—yet scoring a direct hit as in his recent *Oka Oorie Katha* (1977), or *Ek Din Pratidin* (And Quiet Rolls the Dawn, 1979) where he chose a small manageable frame in the village or the city to portray the inevitable defeat of the vulnerable in the present situation. Ritwik in a sense is the most disturbing figure. His films constitute a record of the traumas of change—from the desperation of the rootless and the deprived refugees from East Bengal—*Meghe Dhaka Tara* (The Hidden Star, 1959). *Komal Gandhar* (E Flat, 1960), *Subarnarekha* (1965)—to his verdict on the failure of the Indian Society to function with justice—*Jukti, Takko Aar Gappo* (Reason, Debate and a Tale, 1977).

These men stamped indelibly certain features on the New Cinema. A basic element was their total and instinctive understanding of the common people. Another was their refusal to play the commercial cinema game—drugging of the mind with ersatz emotion, pseudo folk dances (later pop and disco music), contrived situations, "noble" or tough dialogue. A third was their imaginative adaptation of Indian literary classics of writers like Tagore and Prem Chand. Their sensibility was definitely Western. In fact their very objectivity was a child of the West. They used it marvellously to portray the splendours and the tragedies of the country in a native and comprehensible sense—to Indian cinema whose major features till then were acquiescence and placidity.

The "new" film makers of the next generation have displayed an amazing variety of personal attitudes and approaches. And yet, I think, they have paid homage in

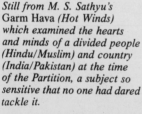

Still from M. S. Sathyu's Garm Hava *(Hot Winds) which examined the hearts and minds of a divided people (Hindu/Muslim) and country (India/Pakistan) at the time of the Partition, a subject so sensitive that no one had dared tackle it.*

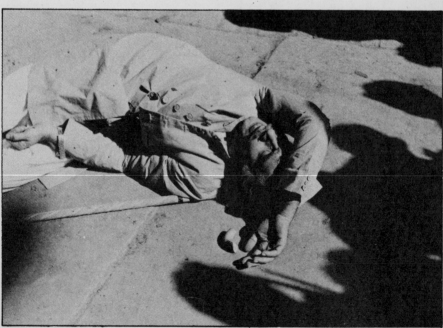

The team of amateurs who came up with Samskara *(Funeral Rites, 1970), a film that put Kannada cinema on the Indian map and gave it its strongly literary and regional emphasis.*

Still from Ek Din Pratidin *(And Quiet Rolls the Dawn) which exposes the tensions of urban middle class life.*

a vital fashion to the elements set out above. At the risk of distortion (and omission) I shall set out five discernible trends.

It was Mani Kaul and Kumar Shahani who led the most notable and conscious revolt against the then current traditions. Their most representative films are Mani's *Uski Roti* (A Day's Bread) and Kumar's *Maya Darpan.* A section of Indian critics has called their cinema "personalised" and criticised their obsession with Bresson. I would relate them to Resnais. Their long takes, their intermingling of past and present, subjective time being mixed up with the story's "now," their overlapping sounds and images—all this is reminiscent of Resnais. There is a rather special way of looking at Indian reality but it is certainly a valid one. They have not yet resolved the major problems posed by this kind of style. But they are the kind of artists who will persist. Our cinema needs their kind of persistence. Their mastery of conventional film making is shown in their documentaries.

Mani's *Arrival* (1981) depicting the converging of animals, vegetables, workers arriving in Bombay's markets into commodities, and Kumar's *Fire in the Belly* (1975) about drought in rural areas, constitute landmarks in the genre.

15

Directors like Shyam Benegal, Mrinal Sen, Girish Karnad, M. S. Sathyu, Ketan Mehta, Mani Kaul and G. Aravindan are heirs not only of the Ray philosophy but also of the social and political conscience of Indian film makers in the 1930's and 40's, and they may be India's best hope of attracting a wider foreign audience, bridging the gap to Western sensibilities while remaining true, as Mr. Ray has done, to an essential Indianness.

Barbara Crossette
The New York Times
June 21, 1981

Shyam Benegal and M.S. Sathyu began as neo-realistic humanists, though that label might seem too constricting today. Sathyu certainly scored a winner with his very first film *Garm Hava* (Hot Winds), the first and upto now the last film to deal credibly with the partition holocaust of 1947. Shyam has displayed a penchant for digging into our feudal and caste relationships and neuroses with verve, imagination and persistence. His touch is assured but a trifle prosy and unambiguous. However, he has shown resource and imagination in film making — badly needed qualities for survival in the commercial jungle.

The film makers of Karnataka — Karanth, Karnad, Reddy, Kasaravalli — raised the banner of New Cinema in the South so distinctively that New Cinema became identified with Regional Cinema. This identification was not entirely correct. Perhaps what was meant was that Regional Cinema "paid" its way. This was due to a happy combination of factors — State subsidies, lower costs of production, a sympathetic market. But regionality is not causally related to New Cinema. What marked the Karnataka School was its preoccupation with the dead yet stultifying ritual, with the oppressive ambience of a specific rural structure. There were also indications of literariness, of an oversharp intellectualism.

This is brought into relief when one turns to

the Kerala School, whose main representatives are Adoor Gopalakrishnan and G. Aravindan—two men who will, I predict, one day rightly inherit Ray's mantle. Despite great variances in their work, there is a common openness to life, a sensuous apprehension of the external world. Whereas Adoor in some respects is a pagan, Aravindan seems to be on the way to becoming a mystic of cinema—a not unworthy relation of Tarkovsky.

As the eighties begin, the New Cinema has brought forth two remarkable films—Nihalani's *Aakrosh* (The Cry of the Wounded) and Mirza's *Albert Pinto*. The first is a smouldering and finally explosive indictment of a ruling structure which has oppressed the tribals. The second is a rather self-consciously Brechtian but original attempt to portray class war in the cities in a dialectical fashion. Their attitude to the current establishment goes far beyond their specific themes. In so far as they attempt, dislocatingly, to alter our perception of current reality they are political films in a very direct sense.

The Indian New Cinema is not an infant. It is too self-conscious and aware to merit that description. It has its difficulties of identification and form, but these are not major ones. What is troubling is its financial struggle to keep alive, to get its message across to the millions, to clear the cobwebs of history, to snap the mind-forged manacles in our land.

State aid in the form of loans and assistance, of proposed art theatres is being considered. But such aid is both limited and, in the long run, a dangerous crutch. The aim of the New Cinema is not merely to make inroads into the commercial cinema audience. If it is to change people, it must propagate a new morality.

In that task it has History on its side. What better patron could it want?

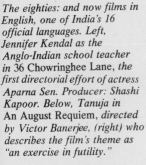

The eighties: and now films in English, one of India's 16 official languages. Left, Jennifer Kendal as the Anglo-Indian school teacher in 36 Chowringhee Lane, *the first directorial effort of actress Aparna Sen. Producer: Shashi Kapoor. Below, Tanuja in* An August Requiem, *directed by Victor Banerjee, (right) who describes the film's theme as "an exercise in futility."*

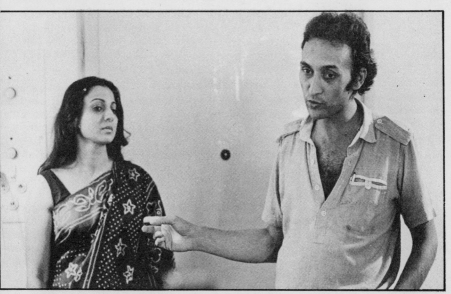

THE FILM FRAMEWORK: GOVERNMENT SUPPORT

The Prime Minister, Shrimati Indira Gandhi, hosted a reception in New Delhi for delegates attending the Eighth International Film Festival of India held in early January, 1981. The Prime Minister is seen here with some of the Jury members.

The New Cinema in India stands for a kind of protest. Yet, its strongest supporter is the government. Few countries in the world have extended as much help and aid to emerging film makers. The motivation is partly the government's aim to discover and disseminate the country's rich sources of cinematic culture. Another reason is the keen competition from State to State, language to language, to prove its cinematic merit as a separate identity.

Dr. Gopal Dutt analyses the ways in which State finance is provided for films made by newcomers or films that may not sell...

TRAINING THE FILM MAKER

In 1960-61, the Government of India established the Film Institute of India at Pune, which in 1971 expanded into the Film and Television Institute of India (FTII). There are two other institutions in Madras and Bangalore, with good training facilities.

The training of film makers at the FTII is comprehensive. The young film makers who took their diplomas this year did a five year stint. In the final year each student studying film direction has to complete an advertisement film, a documentary film, a song picturisation (to equip him for the Indian commercial films) and a 20 minute short, each exercise subsidized entirely by the FTII.

Address: Film and Television Institute of India,
Law College Road,
Pune 4.

THE NATIONAL FILM ARCHIVE OF INDIA

These young film makers are greatly benefitted by the presence of the Archive next door. The NFAI established in 1964, now has a collection of 5744 films from all over the world and it is constantly growing.

Address: The National Film Archive of India,
Jaykar Bungalow,
Law College Road,
Pune 4.

A CHEQUERED CAREER

It is difficult for the newly graduated director to find work. The film industry will employ a trained cameraman, an editor or a sound recordist, but not a fledgling film director. The government-run television, too, is quite willing to employ FTII-trained technicians but is reluctant to take on film direction diploma holders. Given the chance, they could become competent television producers.

There is no sign of an underground film movement either by these trained film makers or enthusiastic amateurs: they cannot afford the high cost of equipment and raw film. The odds against them are heavy.

STATE FINANCING OF GOOD FILMS

Here again the Government of India has come to the rescue. It set up the Film Finance Corporation (FFC) in 1960. The FFC recently merged with the Indian Motion Picture Export Corporation (IMPEC) and is now known as the National Film Development Corporation (NFDC). The FFC-NFDC have financed 133 feature films to date.

LOW BUDGET FOR MORE FREEDOM

One significant aspect of these films is that they are low budgeted. Funds being assured, they are shot in an economical and disciplined manner, according to a planned schedule, and are free from the demands and interference of financiers.

SCRIPT COMMITTEES FOR OBJECTIVITY

NFDC received about 46 scripts last year of which 10 were selected. NFDC's Script Committees scrutinise each script submitted to them with an application. The committees are broad-based to ensure objectivity and comprise 39 members in Bombay, 30 in Madras and 23 in Calcutta.

FILM SCRIPT AWARDS

In 1980, NFDC instituted a script awards competition which attracted 118 entries. Cash awards were given to the winners (selected by a jury) along with the offer to make the winning script into a film as an NFDC production. The 1981 script awards competition drew 179 entries.

PRODUCTION OF FILMS BY NFDC

NFDC have now decided to produce films on their own. Film makers can make their films and earn a fee for their creative work, without being burdened with the problems of distribution and the repayment of loans or incurring a loss.

CO-PRODUCTIONS IN INDIA

Ben Kingsley poses with Govind Nihalani's Second Unit during the filming of Richard Attenborough's Gandhi.

Because of its varied scenery, its cultural panorama and the availability of trained personnel at a lower cost, India has always attracted co-production from other countries. Recently, the government took the lead in co-producing a film titled *Gandhi* being made by Richard Attenborough. It is the biggest budgeted film ever made in India. A few more co-productions, including one with a French company, are being considered.

RAISING AN INFRA-STRUCTURE

Lack of equipment and facilities is a drawback. NFDC is financing many films in 16mm, but re-recording (mixing) facilities in 16mm are not readily available. Projects to supplement the existing NFDC equipment by purchasing 16mm cameras, tape recorders and 16mm editing tables are underway. By working in 16mm the cost of production is considerably reduced.

NFDC will soon instal the first up-to-date subtitling machine in India, which it badly needs considering the multi-lingual character and potential foreign market.

PROBLEMS OF FINANCE

One must laud the Indian government for its help to regional producers which permits the minorities to be heard in their own languages.

Combat (France)
January 18, 1974

Raising funds to finance more films was FFC's main problem. The films that were out of the ordinary could not easily find buyers. Invariably, the loans were not repayed. A major portion of the investment had to be written off as bad debts.

The Government of India then decided to provide FFC with a steady income. A canalisation fee on raw film imported in India and a special Import Licence for buying foreign films stabilized FFC to a large extent. Many of these imported films are not meant for commercial channels and are distributed instead to film societies, university film clubs and welfare groups at subsidized rates.

IMPORTED FILMS

Some of these imported films are totally commercial and are the money spinners. The distribution of these films has made the NFDC self-sufficient and financially sound. They can now finance a number of capable film makers who submit viable scripts.

DISTRIBUTION NETWORK

Many of the FFC (NFDC) financed films have won national and international awards. Most of these films do not reach the audience for whom they are meant. Established distributors do not buy them. When the NFDC tries to place a film in a theatre, the rentals are so high that the release of the film means a further loss.

Only recently, the NFDC has started its own distribution network (mainly with its imported commercial films). They hope to use the network to benefit their own films as well.

FINANCING NEW THEATRES

A scheme for financing the construction of theatres by private entrepreneurs is another effort to aid film making. NFDC will have an option on a part of the playing time in these theatres.

ART CINEMA PROJECTS

But if the New Cinema is to survive and flourish, there is no alternative but to have a chain of art cinemas all over the country. A project with this purpose in mind was started in August 1979. Various State governments and State Film Development Corporations were approached to build low budget, small capacity art cinemas with the help of NFDC. The response was good. Over 30 cinema projects in various State capitals and some other cities are likely to commence.

Address: National Film Development Corporation,
13/16 Regent Chambers,
Nariman Point,
Bombay 400 021.

DIRECTORATE OF FILM FESTIVALS

Yesteryear's film star Devika Rani lights the traditional lamp to inaugurate 'Filmostav 80' in Bangalore.

The Government of India provides sufficient funds to the Directorate of Film Festivals to organise International Film Festivals in India every year. A competitive festival in New Delhi one year is followed by a non-competitive festival the next year at one of India's major film-producing cities. These festivals include a section covering New Cinema in which a selection of 21 Indian films of the year are screened. The Directorate subtitles these films and produces a companion publicity book to highlight the years's cinematic output. Restrospective programs of noted Indian and foreign film directors too are arranged during the festival.

The Directorate arranges for the selection and entry of Indian films to film festivals held in other countries. It also organises international film weeks on an exchange basis.

The Directorate organises the National Film Awards (the most highly valued in India) under which Indian films in various languages and categories are judged annually. Awards are also given to experts in various departments of film making.

Address: The Directorate of Film Festivals,
Lok Nayak Bhavan,
Khan Market,
New Delhi 110 003.

CHILDREN'S FILM SOCIETY

The Society was formed in 1955. It produces feature films and short films for children. It organises subsidized shows and distributes film prints. It also organises an International Children's Film Festival held every other year in India. Its financial support stems mainly from grants given by the Government of India.

Address: Children's Film Society (India),
Hingorani House,
78 Dr. Annie Besant Road, Worli,
Bombay 400 018.

Still from B. V. Karanth's Chor Chor Chup Chup Ja *(Thief, Steal by Quietly), starring Om Puri: a Children's Film Society production*

... I was most impressed with ... Om Puri ... who studied at Poona (and) has nothing of the classic 'jeune premier'...
He is at his best when anguished, and usually is so on screen — there always is ample cause given the tortured plots of most of the films in which he appears.

Elliott Stein
Film Comment (U.S.A.)
July 1981

FILMS DIVISION

Films Division, a department of the Government of India, accounted for approximately 200 short films in 1980. It is perhaps the world's largest single producer and distributor of newsreels and documentaries.

Address: Films Division,
24/G Deshmukh Marg,
Bombay 400 026.

NEW CINEMA AND STATE GOVERNMENTS

In India, cinema mainly falls under the jurisdiction of the individual State governments. Each collects a sizeable tax revenue from cinemas. Almost half of the box-office collections are absorbed by the State government in the shape of Entertainment Tax. The incidence of Entertainment Tax in various States ranges from 37.5% to 157% of the actual ticket price. The State government is therefore obliged to divert part of this considerable revenue for the development of cinema through its State Film Development Corporation. Most of these efforts end up benefiting the film industry and not the quality of a struggling New Cinema. The promotion of good cinema has been mainly left to the Union Government of India which approaches it as a cultural function. Only a few of the State governments have recognised the real needs of the New Cinema.

CONTRIBUTIONS AND CONTRADICTIONS

In West Bengal, New Cinema has been aided by the State government to a large extent. Noted film makers have been given opportunities to make the films they want with the government as producer. A few selected films are given subsidies ranging from Rs. 100,000 to Rs. 300,000.

Several other States provide subsidies and incentives for all the films being made in the local language of the State and shot on its locations or studios. The subsidies differ in quantum from Rs. 50,000 in Kerala to Rs. 150,000 in Karnataka. But they are similar in their non-selective approach. Some of the State governments have realised the futility of subsidising all types of films which only tends to promote mediocrity. But whenever they make a change in favour of a selective subsidy aimed at quality, the lobbies of the commercial cinema pressurise them to maintain the status quo.

In Maharashtra, the government refunds the entire Entertainment Tax earned on a film to the producer, when he is making his next film, upto the extent of Rs. 800,000. In effect, it means that the producer whose film earns the largest profits, gets in addition, a huge grant from public funds. This scheme does not support the struggling aspirant who wants to make his first film or other films despite earlier efforts that have failed at box-office.

In Gujarat, a subsidy of Rs. 25,000 was being granted to the studio where a film was shot. When film makers from all over the world are opting for real locations, the government expected them to return to the studio. Fortunately, this year the policy has been revised to provide for more pragmatic incentives.

Perhaps, a greater awareness amongst administrators and a united effort on the part of film makers will channelise the funds and the energy in individual States for New Cinema to develop in real earnest.

West Bengal government encouraging nationwide film talent: latest in line is M. S. Sathyu with his new film Kahan Kahan se Guzar Gaya *(The Search). Below is a still from the film.*

THE GREATEST

A compulsive mania to busy success marks the Hindi commercial film, which serves as a radar to its keen imitators in other languages of India. The South has outwitted the rest at this game. Now its runaway hits are eagerly adapted into Hindi re-makes.

Vinod Mehta comments on the ramifications of the commercially oriented Hindi film in a country with the world's highest film production.

The commercial cinema in India gets a very bad press. It is constantly attacked for being vulgar, trivial, reactionary, tasteless and exploitative. The response from those on the receiving end of this criticism is usually silence mingled with unconcealed contempt.

The "Industry" spokesmen confess that they have no time for academic discussions, especially with those critics who applaud "art" films playing to nearly empty halls. Indeed, the most distressing aspect of film making in India is the absence of communication between those who make films for the "masses" and those involved in the "parallel" cinema. Both factions are usually at each others' throats

The Indian cinema industry, or the "great Indian cinema bazaar," is the largest in the world. In 1980, as many as 742 feature films were produced in 16 different languages, all Indian of course. It is estimated that in Bombay alone 600 films are on the floor at any given time. Out of this less than 20 percent are completed. It is a risky business, but that doesn't seem to deter anyone.

Still from a recent multi-starrer Shaan *(Splendour) with superstars Amitabh Bachchan and Shashi Kapoor pairing off with Parveen Babi and Bindiya Goswami, all four conducting a dance in a bus. The film is directed by filmdom's wonder boy Ramesh Sippy, who surprised India with its biggest grosser,* Sholay *(Flame).*

In a country like India where cinema is the only mass medium — television still being in its infancy — tempers rise fast in any discussion on the role of cinema in a developing society. However, for the 80 million people who visit theatres every week, there is no controversy: seeing a film is a highpoint of social activity. It is also an occasion for the entire family to get together without any social taboos.

Commercial producers and directors are dedicated to the concept of "family entertainment." Both these words — family and entertainment — are vital in any attempt to understand the aspirations of the commercial cinema in India.

Commercial film makers proclaim loudly that "making the masses happy" is their mission. They say that the average Indian is deeply turmoiled in the woes of survival.

Does a person in this situation want to spend three hours pondering over the intractable problems facing the country? I once asked a Bombay taxi-driver if he had seen a "serious" film on the lives of taxi-drivers. "Why should I," he replied, "I know enough about that kind of thing already."

Commercial film makers love to cite such examples. They declare that they are in the business of providing escape, a few hours of carefree fun and frolic. Vicarious pleasure is better than no pleasure at all. It is a powerful argument.

Manmohan Desai, one of India's most successful commercial film makers, says: "I want people to forget their misery. I want to take them into a dream world where there is no poverty, where there are no beggars,

Laxmikant and Pyarelal; (on either side of maestro Raj Kapoor) the two most successful music directors working in tandem on thirty films at any given time. Their hyphenated names pre-sell a film long before it is shot. Their disc comes first.

Ancient India, unlike Greece, had no tragic drama: how could there be a sense of tragedy when life was *Maya*, illusion or only a transmigratory stage on to another existence? In a curious way the film presented to the illiterate masses a view of the world to which their innermost being responded. And so, without being aware of it, the movie makers became the heirs of the great Sanskrit dramatists.

Reginald Massey
Extract from the Henry Morley Lecture in the Royal Society of Arts Journal (U.K.) May 1974

where fate is kind and god is busy looking after his flock."

The god motif is both strong and inviolable. The wicked are punished and the righteous rewarded. It might take a little time but virtue triumphs in the end.

Interestingly, the god is not always Hindu. In a country where communal passions (usually Hindu-Muslim) are rarely dormant, commercial film makers ensure that obeisance is paid to the government's declared policy of secularism. Followers of Krishna, Allah, Christ, Buddha are all equal, blessed and seen to live in harmony. Naturally there are a few "mischief mongers" but they are quickly dubbed "anti-social" and punished.

Since the commercial cinema has a national following, it cannot have a regional identity. Not surprisingly, then, the sets, costumes, stories, characters have a rootlessness that is distinctive. True, in Hindi films the North Indian ethos dominates, but even here it is difficult to pinpoint any specifics. This deliberate rootlessness is designed to keep all geographical regions happy.

Meanwhile, the "family" aspect means the film must have something for the kids, teenagers, parents and grandparents. To accommodate "something for everybody" means that the average film must contain many diverse elements. The only common denominator is music. Even here the songs (usually six per film) both in terms of words and music, must cater to four generations. The need to string together so many strands accounts for the inordinate length of the commercial film — usually 160 minutes.

Foreign observers are usually amused by the songs in Indian films. There are sound reasons for their inclusion, not as unfamiliar a pattern to Western audiences as it might seem.

First, music is one of the components of family entertainment and takes its place with melodrama, comedy, action, dance etc. Its importance is reflected in the credits: the music director's name appears close to the director's. Frequently on bill-boards it is the only name mentioned. A film's market value partly depends on its music and lyrics. Laxmikant-Pyarelal, the most successful music-director team, reportedly work on 30 movies simultaneously.

A more important, though less obvious, reason for the mandatory presence of songs is that they help break up conflict and tension, whether religious, social or sexual. If this tension is not resolved then the film strays into areas beyond the commercial film maker's control. It might even enter into areas of realism, something which he must avoid at all costs. For example, male-female sexuality has never been honestly explored or presented. A strict censorship policy has not a little to do with this ambivalence. Whenever a film approaches genuine passion, the director funks and takes refuge in melody. Sex is a controversial, unpredictable emotion and he is not certain how audiences will respond. The public and the stars are equally averse to kissing being shown on

Aruna Irani, the appealing screen seductress who specializes in jazzing up traditional dance forms in Indianised cabaret items, like this one.

Amitabh Bachchan, the most phenomenally successful star ever to appear on the Indian screen. Tall, lanky, stunning he-man and smouldering lover, here he cuddles and sings to one of his regular heroines, Raakhee.

screen just as the national policy tends to be on the subject.

No discussion on the commercial Indian cinema is complete without an examination of the "star" system. This system has always existed and is currently at its peak.

The deities of the Indian Cinema are its stars. As they were in the heyday of Hollywood. Their life-style and invented substance fill countless magazines, provide models for social aspirations, are even the springboard for political clout (M. G. Ramachandran, currently Chief Minister of Tamil Nadu and his arch rival Annadurai crossed swords in screenplays to promote political premises; no presidential TV debate, but based on the power of the fictional art and thrust of feature films).

Most stars in India are male. Commercial film makers make no bones about the fact that this is a male dominated industry. The heroines are usually appendages, their role little beyond being decorative. A well-known producer confessed recently that he would never make a film "revolving around a woman." "It just," said the producer, "wouldn't sell, the masses won't accept it." Incidentally, this claim has never been seriously tested on the screen.

Today the biggest star in India is Amitabh Bachchan. It is estimated that currently 750 million rupees of industry money have been invested in him. If his popularity falls, as it has been doing lately, the "industry will collapse." No one in India knows how much Mr. Bachchan is paid per film. However, it is known that his fee alone can comprise half the cost of the production. The average cost of a commercial Hindi film is seven and a half million rupees. The multi-starrer can cost five times as much. A star sells a film as nothing else does, each booked well in advance against a token "signing" amount. And each may have 30 films on hand at one time. The stars work two to three even four shifts a day, with only one shift being given to each film. The day can also squeeze in the compulsory recording sessions.

All sound in Indian films is dubbed subsequent to

Kalpana Iyer, a younger contender for the role of the hip-swinging screen vamp, adapting the disco trend to Indo-Anglian words. This still is of her dancing to a hit tune called "Hari Om Hari."

shooting. The reasons could be that crowd and street sounds cannot be controlled. At times, the cameras used are not self-blimped. A few still use optical sound tracks because of a lack of infrastructure in many centres. Again a star on multi-shifts does not know his lines and conventional scripts are not written. Mouthing sound to action allows for more effective and expedient "faking" and is cheaper in the long run.

With so much at stake with each star, the film industry breathes and lives with each one. If a Parveen Babi or Sanjeev Kumar falls ill (they have for prolonged periods) or Amjad Khan has an accident, around twenty films can come to a grinding halt. No wonder multi-starrers take years—five to ten at times—to complete, which accounts for the structure of financing being so shaky.

Financiers often invest in "steps." Usually the "hero" is signed first. If he is a big enough name, potential distributors pay a deposit for distribution rights. A song or two is recorded and played for financiers or distributors—some more money may be forthcoming. Thus the film is completed. It is an unhappy arrangement and directors have been known to resign due to "interference" from "outside elements" which usually means financiers.

There is some talk currently about "civilising" the commercial cinema. Critics acknowledge that its motivations are beyond change. What can be done is to "smoothen the rough edges."

Commercial film makers themselves concede the need for "civilising." By this they mean a more vigorous and thorough approach to craft and technique. As a result the commercial cinema in the last few years has become vastly more professional and directors like Yash Chopra, Subhash Ghai, Manmohan Desai and Ramesh Sippy are admired by the supporters of the parallel cinema for "style."

Nothing else is likely to change. Why should it? Commercial cinema makers in India feel they are socially "responsible" and "useful," as they provide sorely needed diversion to the "toiling masses." And what, they ask, does the "art" cinema provide? Despair, defeat, hopelessness and introspection. The war goes on.

India's ace director, Manmohan Desai (straw-hatted) relaxes with top stars Jeetendra (left) and Dharmendra (right) during the shooting of his gladiatorial saga, Dharam Veer (Two Brothers).

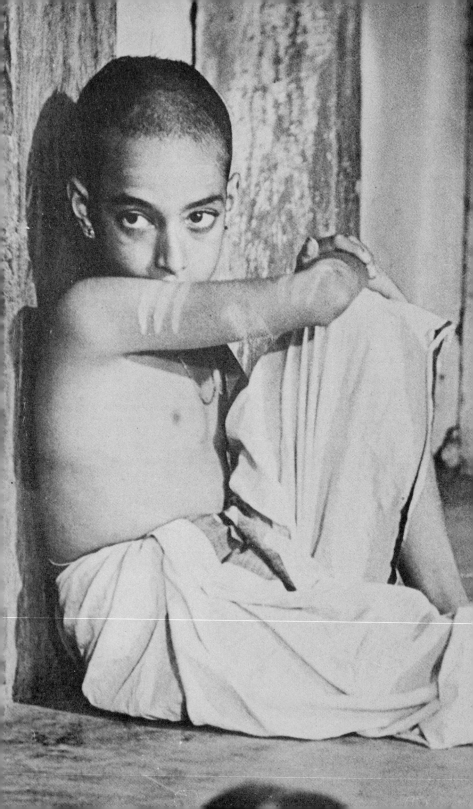

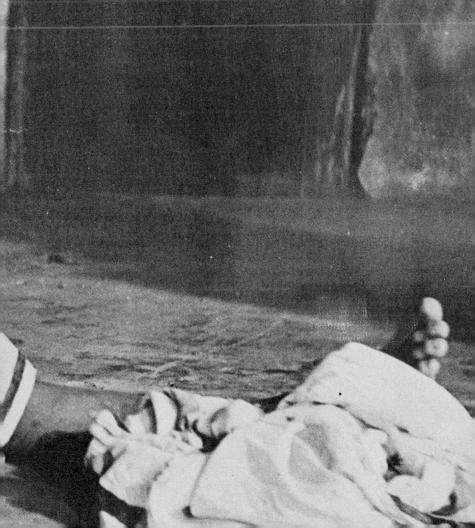

THE INDIAN ETHOS

One of India's most noted features is its interplay of bewildering contrasts. The country is known as one where past and present co-exist. The people of today express their tradition and beliefs in a variety of contradictory ways that can puzzle the viewer. And the country's New Cinema conveys behavioral and cultural patterns more graphically than any other art form.

M. V. Kamath presents a perceptive insight into the subtle nuances that characterize the Indianness of New Indian Cinema.

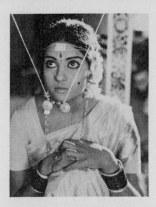

The mangalsutra, *the sacramental thread, is placed round the bride's neck, sealing her fate for better or worse.*

The new bride touches the feet of her mother-in-law, as a mark of respect, and to seek her blessings.

Previous page:
Nani, the novice initiated into brahminical learning in Girish Kasaravalli's Ghatashraddha *(The Ritual). The horizontal caste-marks indicate that he belongs to the* shaivite *sect.*

Commercial cinema, like death and income tax has always been with us. But the parallel cinema comes to India and, one hopes, goes abroad like a breath of fresh air. It is Indian to the core. But what, it may be asked, is so Indian about the New Indian Cinema? For that matter we may well raise another question: what's so Indian about Indians? How do they differ from any other people? What are their individual, collective and societal characteristics? Is it possible, truly, to understand and appreciate India's parallel cinema without understanding the country's social and cultural ethos? The answer in such a situation is both yes and no.

Any sensitive individual, no matter how foreign to the Indian situation *can* to some extent empathise with it. But for a total understanding of the parallel Indian cinema, a total immersion in the "Indianness" of India may be necessary.

This need not put off even the casual viewer. Some aspects of the parallel cinema are easily explained. For instance, the slow pace of the film. Satyajit Ray exploited it fully, but one suspects that it came naturally to him. His aim, evidently, was to explore the "innerness" or the interior landscape of people, the camera gently resting at length on the sadness of faces, the indrawing of objects or the eternity of landscape.

It is true, the Indian is more introspective than most Westerners. In a rural setting, where silence seems to be all-embracing, and life itself slow, the director would be out of tune with his theme if his pace seemed forced. Very often, music and songs with their lyrics, are discreetly blended with the visuals to underline their impact.

The persistent practice of ritual carries meaning to an Indian audience that may escape the attention of a Western viewer. An individual's caste is expressed — and noticed — in many significant ways: in dress, deportment, body marks, in attitudes, all of which call for sustained attention. Indeed the viewer is invited to notice the many allusions to social mores (caste marks on the body, the absence of the customary red dot on the woman's forehead, indicating widowhood *or* a state of being unworthy of the sanctity of marriage: the folds of a man's flowing robes, etc.) which will tell him at a glance the context of the film.

Interestingly enough, the very complexity of the Indian mosaic makes it difficult for one Indian to know another as he would like to. Though superficially Indians may be alike, each of the twenty-two States and nine Union Territories has an indigenous culture of its own. Each minority has its own communication system that may not always be apparent to an alien group. Yet there are value systems that cut across ethnic barriers. Today's New Cinema reflects all these.

The Indian often speaks with his body. His body language is different from that of the Westerner. Both obedience and obeisance have their own nuances that may not always be apparent to someone from an alien culture.

Respect for the older generation is ritualised by touching the feet of the elders as a greeting as well as to seek their blessing. The eyes of an Indian may veil a gamut of emotions because a code of conduct preempts voicing a feeling or opinion. Women are traditionally silent, docile and unobtrusive, before men in particular. The ostracised young wife in *Sara Akash* (The Whole Sky), is allowed no vocal or other protest against her unbearable situation. Her reactions are in her eyes, her gestures and her hidden tears. But in Kerala State the situation is different: it follows a matrilineal system. The neglected wife in *Kodiyettam* (Ascent), lashes out at her lackadaisical husband before she leaves him in disgust.

Kissing on screen is taboo. It can be suggested as strongly as possible but not shown. Even in their daily lives, Indians are openly demonstrative only with children.

Another Indian tradition is the respect and rectitude the younger generation must observe before elders. An Indian youth may not smoke or drink before his parents. Obedience is imperative and one cannot talk back, no matter what. The working girl in Sen's *Ekdin Pratidin* (And Quite Rolls the Dawn), maintains a defiant silence when accused unjustly and insultingly of impropriety.

The parallel cinema, intentionally or not, is India's cinema realite. It holds a mirror to the Indian society and shows it as it is. There is little, if any, that is contrived. Many are films that attempt at protest against oppression of all kinds: social, economic, even political.

The feudal oppression of the tribals living in the forests comes through with appalling clarity in *Aakrosh* (Cry of the Wounded). In *Samskara* (Funeral Rites), we are exposed to the tyranny of caste.

The reality of India assails us at every flick of a frame, in its urban-rural contradictions: the depravity of people uprooted from their homes, as in *Chakra* (Vicious Circle), or urban isolation, as in *27 Down.* Go a step further to *Albert Pinto Ko Gussa Kyon Aata Hai* (What Makes Albert Pinto Angry), and you see the agonies of a man dissatisfied with everything he sees around him and his hope of going to what he conceives as the ultimate paradise, Canada. Albert Pinto belonging to the small Christian minority is true to a certain type.

One could call these films of protest—protest against a situation peculiar to India. The triumph of social

elf-imposed censorship; thus ar and no further: physical ntimacy between the sexes nay be suggested but ot shown.

Looking for inspiration in folk forms: tamasha, *the suggestive dance of Maharashtra with overtones of topical commentary.*

dogmatism over humanism is the theme of *Ghatashraddha* (The Ritual). Here is a vignette from India of the South and an India of brahmins — a minority. Or take M. S Sathyu's *Garm Hava* (Hot Winds), reflecting Hindu Muslim tensions, again a peculiarly Indian theme.

Caste rules, often so rigid that breaking them would mean social excommunication if not worse, again, are peculiar to India. Religious tensions, primarily between the Muslim and Hindu, are not to be witnessed in any other country save India where their clashes have historica roots. These clashes and attempts at their resolution acquire an emotional impact that sometimes is traumatic Some twenty years after it first began as a movement of little or no significance, the New Cinema is gathering force and momentum.

The producer of the New Cinema is looking at life with clear eyes and comes up with many surprises. India *is* a country of surprises. Not all Indians can pick up suggestions, symbolic or otherwise, often important to the understanding of a film, because of the very complexity of the country with its many levels of culture, education and it class and caste distinction. If this is a cause for despair at least the foreign viewer can relax in the knowledge that Indians, too, could be strangers to each other.

What is significant about the New Cinema is the effort of its makers to approach the filmgoer in his own language and culture. If this calls for the use of the forms of the performing arts, that too is done. The aim is not just to touch the filmgoer's imagination, but stimulate his comprehension. New Cinema talks to him directly, shorn of artificiality by showing him his world in its grim facets The message induces self-recognition in the viewer. He may *want* to identify himself with the characters in commercial cinema, but with those in the New Cinema the identification is almost instantaneous. He sees in them not what he may want to be but what he *is*. This is at once the power and the prestige of the New Cinema.

India is where contradiction is, where synthesis is where variety is, where there also is a deadening uniformity of beliefs and dogma. In the midst of all this are the efforts of those who try to rise above the superstition and the fear, to heights of a personal freedom that is meaningful to them.

Under the Indian "calm" lives a daily storm vibrant with movement, passion, anger, violence. This comes through powerfully in the New Cinema. Nothing is taken for granted. Everything is allowed to surface, whether as in Mrinal Sen's *Bhuvan Shome* or Shyam Benegal's *Bhumika* (The Role), and very powerfully as in *Aakrosh* (Cry Of The Wounded).

The New Cinema shatters the tourist view of India as a passive, exotic, idyllic country content to shuffle along. I shows another and truer India, not mysterious but living and continuously striving to fuse its splintered fragment into an ordered totality.

THE LONG AND SHORT OF IT

Indian documentaries started out as the Information Films of India. The Films Division of today remains an arm of the Government, spreading news and information to the people. However, FD does utilise the talents of promising freelance film makers of the country. Besides, State Governments and private industry, among others, are beginning to sponsor a small independent documentary movement.

B. D. Garga traces the history of the documentary film in India.

Still from Vinod Chopra's Encounter with Faces, a short film about children placed in homes for the destitute.

In his book, 'Documentary — A History of the Non-fiction Film', Erik Barnouw writes: "When German armies drove into Poland in September 1939, they plunged also into the film genre that was to dominate documentary production throughout World War II: the bugle-call films adjunct to military action, weapon of war."

About this time, the British in India were in search of some device to persuade the antagonistic Indians to participate in the war. In the hostile atmosphere of India's growing nationalism, film offered both a defensive and offensive medium. So it seemed to Desmond Young, an official in the Department of Information at Delhi (who was later to write several books, among them the best-seller 'Rommel'). He asked the Ministry of Information London, to send over a documentary film maker. So it was that late in 1940 the Film Advisory Board, later known as Information Films of India, was set up, with the British film maker Alexander Shaw as its first producer.

It was not easy to make official films at that particular time of India's history when the sub-continent was seething with discontent. Indian audiences walked out of a theatre as soon as a war propaganda film came on the screen. But as the IFI started to produce films relevant to Indian life, especially films on agriculture, industry, public health, architecture, handicrafts, educational and cultural subjects, their interest was revived. Particularly the cultural films awakened interest and pride in India's own heritage and accomplishments among both urban and rural audiences.

The Indian film maker too was exposed for the first time to the series, *March of Time* and the war films of Frank Capra, John Huston, William Wyler, Jonis Ivens, Alberto Cavalcanti, John Grierson, Harry Watt, Humphrey Jennings and Paul Rotha. He was jolted into the realisation that cinema was not just the meretricious fare he was used to. It could be an effective means of communication in our vast country with its heterogenous character.

The aftermath of global war, and the dissolution of colonialism that followed, was to create in many parts of the world, especially in Asia, new tensions and fresh opportunities. A film unit became "an expression of nationhood, a chronicler of achievements."

After independence in 1947, the national government approved a scheme for continuing the work of the IFI. It set up the Films Division in 1948 to produce films "for public information, education, motivation and for institutional and cultural purposes." The Films Division started with a modest program, producing 36 documentaries and 52 newsreels annually. It now produces about 120 documentaries and 52 editions of the national newsreel. Most of these films are initially made in English or Hindi and later dubbed in the 14 major Indian languages. It supplies about 50,000 prints of its films every year for commercial and non-commercial distribution. About 70 million people see its documentaries and newsreels each week in the country's 10,500 theatres.

The exhibition of these films has been made compul-

Jean Bhownagary, leading documentary film maker who gave an impetus to the short film movement during the sixties.

Paul Zils, Fali Bilimoria and S. Sukhdev, pioneers of the documentary film.

Still from Through the Eyes of a Painter *by M. F. Husain.*

sory through an Act of Parliament. Thus the Films Division has a ready-made exhibition network throughout the country. It produces films on a wide range of subjects concerning art, culture, industry, science, education, agriculture, health and hygiene.

Despite the supervisory eye of officialdom, some film makers surprisingly do manage to make their individual statements. Here I must digress to pay tribute to the German film maker Paul Zils, who made India his home and continued to enrich the Indian documentary movement for nearly two decades. He has an impressive body of work to his credit. In addition, he trained a number of Indian technicians and directors, prominent among them, Fali Bilimoria and Sukhdev.

To return to the Films Division. It learned from the experience of wartime IFI, of the popularity of cultural and art films. While it made a number of films on the cave paintings of Ajanta, the sculptures of Ellora, the temples of Bodh Gaya and the rock

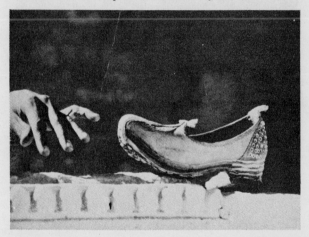

temples of South India, it was not until the production of *Khajuraho* (directed by Mohan Wadhwani and produced by Jean Bhownagary) that the art film in India came into its own. The extensive Khajuraho complex of temples in Central India has evoked worldwide interest largely due to the unsurpassed excellence of its erotic sculpture. The camera looks at the temples wonder-eyed with the reverence of a devotee, the passion of a lover, traversing the whole length of the richly ornate ceilings, sliding along the arches holding figures of deities, musicians, celestial maidens, *mithuna* (the amorous couples "where each is both") and ascetics doing penance.

Konarak, yet another striking film, was made by P. Dasgupta, who died tragically young and had worked with Claude Renoir. He studied film making in the United States. It should perhaps be mentioned that many of the young film makers — K.L. Khandpur, Mushir Ahmed, Jagat Murari, Ramakantha Sarma, Ravi Prakash — who joined the Films Division in 1948 were trained in American film

A purificatory dip in the holy river from Women of India *by Fali Bilimoria.*

schools. Among these was Arun Chowdhary who made a very evocative film *The Jain Temples*. He kept his camera constantly on the move, closing in on a detail now, gliding over rows of delicately carved figures and then suddenly whirling about the pendant of the temple's dome. When asked to explain what seemed like a pre-occupation with movement, Chowdhary said, "It is simple. The sculpture, though it suggested movement, could not move. So I let the camera do that."

Clement Baptista, a veteran documentary film maker, shot a brilliant film *Kailash at Ellora*, designed to demonstrate the unique feat of rock carving perfected more than a thousand years ago. Jainism, Buddhism and Hinduism, age-old and inherent creeds of the country, which have inspired some of the most outstanding art and architecture anywhere in the world, was a challenge and an inspiration for the film maker.

Painting too has existed in India since the dawn of its artistic history. In the 2000-year-old frescoes of Ajanta, the monk painters told the story of the Buddha in a variety of forms, vibrant with life. Up in the foothills of the Himalayas in small native states, miniature painting continued to flourish into the 17th and 18th centuries. The love life of Krishna as sung in their folk songs, greatly fascinated the *Pahari* (hill) painters and found expression in their sensitive, reticent and tender work. Jean Bhownagary was quick to sense its filmic possibilities and produced *Radha and Krishna,* a film based on these paintings. It brings alive the poetry of the miniatures, their delicate colouring, with great sensitivity. Bhownagary followed it up with another film, *Akbar,* on the great Moghul.

Naturally, films were produced on modern contemporary painters. Santi Chowdhury made films on the paintings of Tagore, Husain and Paritosh Sen. Satyajit Ray paid an eloquent tribute to his teacher Binode Bihari in *The Inner Eye*. This author made a film on the first modern painter of India, *Amrita Shergil,* who died at the age of 28 and whose work inspired a whole generation of Indian painters.

In recent years, the Indian film maker's concern has shifted to more immediate socio-economic issues and political complexities. The earliest films in this genre were Sukhdev's *After the Eclipse,* and *And Miles to Go —* both films of engaging polemics, a style he was to perfect and sharpen in his later work like *Nine Months to Freedom* on the birth of Bangladesh, and *After the Silence* on bonded labour. Sukhdev's most celebrated work was *India '67* (now called *An Indian Day*) a fascinating collage of impressions of Indian life, remarkable for its keen observations and wealth of detail. A few films that stand out for their bold and refreshing statements are Films Division's *Framework of Famine* and *Report on Drought* on the Bihar famine, Sastry's *I am Twenty* on Indian youth, Chari's *Face to Face* on Indian democracy, and Anand Patwardhan's *Prisoners of Conscience*.

An Indian Day, *originally made for 'Expo '67', Canada, where it won a top award.*

ali Bilimoria's The House
at Ananda Built, one of the
rst documentaries to
escribe realistically the life
f an Indian farmer.

About this time Fali Bilimoria produced a moving document in *The House that Ananda Built,* a film about a Bihari peasant family and the generation gap that inevitably but imperceptibly creeps in. The film won its maker an Oscar nomination. Bilimoria followed it up with another film, *The Last Raja* on the decline and decay of the feudal system in a princely State. Shyam Benegal, who went on to become a feature film maker made *A Child of the Streets* on vagrant and destitute children. This theme was more eloquently projected in Vinod Chopra's *Encounter with Faces,* which was nominated for an Oscar. Mani Kaul, another feature film maker who had earlier made documentaries on Rajasthani nomad puppeteers, and the shadow players of Konkan (*Chitrakathi*), has recently made a film on Bombay, *Arrival.* It is remarkable for its searing imagery (its abattoir sequence strangely reminiscent of Georges Franju's *Le Sang des Betes*) and contrapuntal sound track.

There is increasing evidence of much exciting work being done by the young film makers trained at the Film and Television Institute at Pune.

But the tragedy of the Indian documentary is its dependence on official agencies both for sponsorship and release outlets. Government agencies and administrative red tape consort ill with creative imagination and, not infrequently thwart it. Television which has sustained and revolutionised documentary film making in Europe and America, has not as yet provided similar opportunities (or shall we say challenge) to the Indian film maker. These are not insurmountable odds. Satyajit Ray produced his masterpiece in the face of such adversity. And hopefully the Indian documentary will too.

THE DIRECTORS
THEIR FILMS

The directors of the New Indian Cinema work to control everything. The script, art direction, casting, music, camera, editing, and of course production and even the promotion and selling of the film. They gather people around them who share the same values about the purpose of the low budget New Cinema produced with constraints on equipment and laboratory facilities. They are professionally trained in their craft like many of the new actors who want to set superior standards by working in these films for less money. These young directors shoot on real locations, often with a 16 mm camera, more economical and flexible, allowing the film to be blown up to 35 mm for commercial release. Most of these films are funded by State loans.

Distribution and exhibition, monopolised by big time operators whose films are pre-sold to theatres, are a desperate hurdle. Publicity costs are lethal. Luckily some big stars realise the value of acting in these films thus attracting more producers.

Although Hindi is the dominant language with the obvious commercial advantage of being the most widely understood language of the country, the new directors are able to express something unique to their regions in their own language. Hindi understandably happens to be the language of many of their films; they use it as unconventionally as they do the regional languages.

The Review section that follows deals with 19 directors who have contributed to the New Indian Cinema of today. Presented here are profiles of the directors, their filmographies, and synopses of films that have achieved — or deserve — an international viewing.

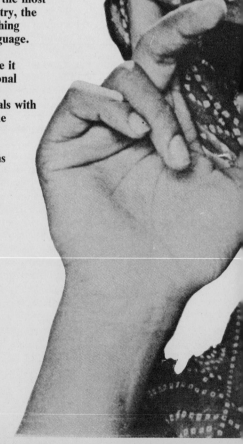

G. ARAVINDAN

Aravindan is a painter, cartoonist, writer, musician and — disconcertingly — Kerala Rubber Board Administrator. He is clearly incapable of producing a clumsy or careless image. He brings the same reverence to landscapes as to people; and his films know no villains. Already he is a director from whom each new work is an event, and it is good to see that he has won swift recognition at home as well as abroad.

Derek Hill
Sight and Sound (U.K.)
Spring 1980

Aravindan, an overwhelmingly large and bearded man in his early forties, was born at Kottayam, the district capital of Kerala's spice and rubber heartland. He was raised in a neighbouring village, and he mourns its passing because small towns have replaced what he remembers as so typical of Kerala.

It was later, as a Biology student in Trivandrum, the State capital, that he was first introduced to cinema. He recalls seeing Kurosawa's *Rashoman* several times. There were no film schools then to nurture his new-found interest. He turned to painting and drawing cartoons instead.

He travelled extensively in the lush countryside of Kerala—an experience of character and landscape which influenced his art.

After graduation, he joined the Rubber Board, a Government department, where he has continued, surprisingly enough, to work till today. It was then that he created his popular cartoon serial, 'Small Men and Big World,' for a well-known Malayalam weekly.

The gift of cartooning was perhaps inherited from his father, an eminent humorist of his time. Aravindan's serial became a literary institution. It drew on the life and tribulations of Ramu, a middle class young man with idealistic and romantic inclinations who takes life all too seriously. Ramu's introspective progress through the world of bourgeois Kerala came to an end soon after Aravindan took to making films.

Aravindan says very quietly (which is his style) but with a noticeable pride and defiance (also his style), "I've never stepped foot in a film school ... not even as a visitor." This was some years ago. He has since been honoured in film campuses here and abroad, as chief guest and more.

Aravindan learnt the craft of film making with surprising speed and ease. Technically his films are strikingly competent. As effortlessly, he seems to have found the kind of producer most film makers dream about. Aravindan's financier on all his films has been the staunch and loyal Ravindran, who runs a family business based on their cashew nut crop. Ravindran is an old associate of Aravindan's over years of a common interest in writing and the theatre. From start to finish, Ravindran does not interfere or intrude in Aravindan's filming. Nor does he make demands on box-office returns. This unusual producer-director relationship continues undiminished by the success—or occasional failure—of Aravindan's prolific output.

Aravindan almost willed himself to become a film maker. He learned as he worked, lighting, editing and much else. He did something more. He gathered round him some of the best young graduates from the Film Institute of India, most of them in their twenties, a group that was to be a powerful asset in his subsequent career and success.

The transition from cartoon to cinema was so smooth that it belied the controversy it raised for Aravindan, the film maker. An embittered social criticism, a nostalgia for private realities, a strong sense of individuality had been conveyed through his cartoons for a decade. It was followed by an uncompromising cinema which departed stylistically from tradition with a vengeance. The result was that even in the progressive Malayalam film culture, Aravindan was branded an "extremist."

Undeterred, Aravindan's subsequent films were marked by a stark purity, pervaded with a lyrical passion, and almost unapproachable in their distance from "Extreme" or even "Middle" cinema in Kerala. In doing so, he gained as many admirers as detractors. To a society searching for its bearings, an overwhelming visual experience like film can have a tremendous impact. Aravindan's work snow-balled into an evergrowing hardcore of good cinema fanatics in Kerala.

Aravindan, the true sage, gives no clue to his reactions. He is an intense and reserved person whose moods surface mostly in his films. The public image of a man of few words is deceptive. He is a warm friend and compassionate human being who often expresses himself more through a suffocating bear-hug. He defends his work vigorously among friends.

Even now, his first love is music. His gatherings invariably turn into impromptu music sessions. Those who consider him withdrawn or shy would be surprised to see him singing with abandon. Aravindan studied *Hindustani* (North Indian) classical music for five years. He is equally knowledgeable about *Carnatac* (South Indian) music. This is reflected not only in the musical scores of his films but also in their rhythm and flow.

While his films are marked by emotional detachment and ambiguity, Aravindan is sentimental and loyal to his friends and his family. The name of his wife Leela features in his cartoon series, while his son Ramu is the central character.

A concern for people is part of his contemplative cinematic style. He has utmost respect for his actors. Many directors use the camera to look more sharply at a person than the person can see himself. The camera becomes an instrument of detection. Aravindan uses the camera to wait patiently until a person communicates his condition. Characteristically, he will hold a shot while an emotion rises to the surface and culminates in a glance or a gesture: actor and viewer both must wait for the emotion to emerge. Simultaneously, a viewer perceives an emotion as the actor expresses it.

Marginal characters are fully humanised in Aravindan's semi-documentary films. The most striking example would be the interaction between the inhabitants of a village and the visiting performers of a circus in *Thampu* (The Circus Tent). Even mysticism does not denude them of their essential humanity. *Esthappan* (Stephen), is the story of an enigmatic and spiritual vagabond. Take the closing shot: Esthappan sleeping by the sea, arms pillowing his head, knees drawn up, frail in sleep like any other man.

Aravindan has the artist's gift of endowing his people with an inner life. He portrays the landscape of Kerala and all its moods with the vision of a poet. For him nature is not just a beautiful backdrop; it becomes an active participant in the narrative.

Aravindan is actively engaged with a folk theatre group. He is one of the eminent directors of a powerful theatre movement in Kerala. His varied artistic pursuits seem to enrich, not dissipate creativity.

Aravindan continues on his compulsively personal path of cinema. His alarmingly Marxian beard and fierce appearance is a poor guard for the warm, unassuming, generous and, above all, gentle person that he is.

V. K. Madhavan Kutty

Comparisons between the two leading Malayalam directors, Aravindan and Gopalakrishnan, are inevitable, and in fact, called for. While Gopalakrishnan belongs to the classically rooted school of realism in cinema, Aravindan is more of a modern impressionist in his approach. Each of Aravindan's films is markedly different in theme and style. He veers sharply from being elliptical, abstract, symbolic to being evocatively descriptive. He has the daring of the fervent convert to improvise and proliferate at will. In seven years he has made five films. He seems to be headed towards making one film every year (apart from documentaries in between).

Aravindan: self portrait

KANCHANA SITA
(Golden Sita)

1977/Colour/87 mins/Malayalam
Direction/Screenplay
G. Aravindan
Produced by
Ravindran Nair
Camera
Shaji
Music
Rajiv Taranath
Editing
Ramesh
Art Direction
Namboodri
Players
Ramdas (Rama),
Venkateshwarlu (Lakshmana),
Chinnapuliah (Bharata),
Keshav Panicker (Valmiki)
Enquiries
General Pictures, Thejes
Jaya Mansion Compound,
Trivandrum, Kerala.

Urmila, Laxmana's wife, pleads with Rama to be more compassionate towards Sita his own sinned-against wife.

Kanchana Sita is based on the Hindu epic 'Ramayana'. Its oldest text is attributed to the first century poet Valmiki. It is the story of a king who has four sons by three wives. The eldest is Rama, the next Lakshmana, the third Bharata, the youngest Shatrughana. Rama wins Sita as his wife after he strings a bow too heavy for a human to lift. The kingdom rejoices in their heir apparent. Bharata's mother covets the throne for her own son. She conspires to have Rama exiled for 14 years. Sita and Lakshmana voluntarily accompany him. A sorrowing and innocent Bharata is left to administer the kingdom.

Towards the end of their sojourn, Sita is abducted by Ravana, demon king of Sri Lanka. Rama with an army of men and monkeys defeats him in battle. The victorious Rama rejects Sita, doubting her chastity during captivity. Sita invokes a trial by fire and proves her innate inviolability. Rama thus accepts her as his queen. They bring peace and prosperity to their kingdom.

Aravindan's film is based on a version of this story in which citizens doubt Sita despite the fire ritual. Gossip leads Rama to abandon her to uphold his kingly office, although he personally believes she is blameless. Sita, humiliated more so because she is pregnant, throws herself in the River Ganges. And she gives birth to twin sons, Lava and Kusa. The river offers them to the poet sage Valmiki who is composing an epic on Rama but cannot envisage its ending.

The film opens with the brothers Rama and Lakshmana entering Dandaka forest in search of the low caste Sambooka. Rama has come to slay him for performing austerities reserved for brahmins alone.

Sita (never seen in the film) is represented by the spirit of Nature and its movement and sounds. She is ever present. Those close to Rama think him callous in his rejection of Sita. Lakshmana's wife, Urmila, speaks bitterly of Rama's majesty. Bharata chastises his brother for dismissing Sita so summarily. Rama says little in reply.

The holy sage Vasistha tells Rama to commence the horse sacrifice, the noblest rite a king can perform. A white horse is let loose to wander at will. The path he follows is by right the king's dominion.

Valmiki's two pupils, Lava and Kusa, chase the horse to their hut. A soldier reports to Rama that the horse is missing. Lakshmana sees Lava guarding the horse. The boy raises his bow to defend his right over his new-found property. Lakshmana does likewise. But the forest rustles with the gentle presence of Sita, thereby restoring harmony.

Touched by the reunion, Valmiki in ecstasy composes the concluding chapter of the 'Ramayana'.

The white horse returns; Rama's authority has been acknowledged. Sambooka is ready for his penance; he must be killed. Valmiki brings Lava and Kusa to the ritual. The forest rustles again. Rama recognises his sons.

All three turn to watch the sacrificial enclosure which is now consigned to flames. Rama cries out in longing for Sita and the boys, as wisps of burned leaves rise into the air. Sita, as Nature, is sublime. Rama begins his endless journey, holding fire in his hand, going towards the river.

Aravindan's film explores two themes. Rama's extreme sense of duty and the driving inspiration of poetry. Aravindan humanises the powerful Rama despite his cold-

Kanchana Sita, **visually breathtaking, though elusive in narrative, daringly depicts the divine personages as prehistoric, black-skinned tribals.**

David Robinson,
The Times (U.K.)
(reporting on
Filmotsav '78, Madras)

ness and unbending rectitude. Rama is haunted by memories of Sita and her divine virtues. Nor does Valmiki unravel Rama's ambiguity. As a poet he is obsessed with completing his life's mission.

Mythologicals are the oldest genre in Indian cinema. Stories from the 'Ramayana' and the 'Mahabharata' tend to be devotional spectacles. Aravindan's contribution is to introduce a contemplative style to an epic genre. He uses the tribals of Andhra Pradesh to portray the mythic characters. The tribals, called *Rama chenchus,* consider themselves descendents of the original Rama.

Satti Khanna

Filmography

1974 UTTARAYANAM (Throne of Capricorn)
B&W/118 mins/Malayalam
Lead Players: D. R. Mohandas, Kunju,
Balan K. Nair, Adoor Bhasi, Sukumaran
Uttarayanam is inspired by Aravindan's own cartoon series exposing opportunism and hypocrisy set against the back drop of the Independence struggle. It is an ironic tale of an alienated unemployed youth confronted with the story of his father who gave his life to the freedom movement. It concludes that making a choice is inevitable.

1977 KANCHANA SITA (Golden Sita)

1978 THAMPU (The Tent)
B&W/130 mins/Malayalam
Lead Players: Gopi, Venu, D. P. Nair, Sreeraman

Thampu is almost a documentary film in its fidelity but imbued with poetic charm. The film probes the tense and lonely lives of the artists of a little circus that pitches its tent in a small village where brief relationships are formed, which end with the end of the visit itself.

Its main interest is in creating a sense, through its images, of the tragi-comedy of life. It is a compassionate film, moving in its intensity.

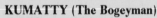

KUMATTY (The Bogeyman)
Col/90 mins/Malayalam
Lead Players: Ramunni, Master Ashokan, Vilasini
Kumatty is the mysterious wizard who stalks children's lore in North Kerala. One day the wizard arrives in person in a remote village out of the twilight of the myths and is soon entrenched among the children as their friendly magician, singer and dancer. There is some confusion when a boy, transformed into a dog, gets lost. But all ends well and Kumatty departs into his shadowy world. As in his other films, Aravindan tells the story by weaving his images into the beauty of nature.

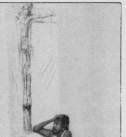

1979 ESTHAPPAN (Stephen)

Col/94 mins/Malayalam
Lead Players: Rajan Kakkanadan, Father Francis David,
Krishnapuram Leela, Sudharama

Set against the backdrop of the Christian fisherfolks' life on the coast of Kerala, the film presents an eccentric and mysterious man called Esthappan who evades definitions and descriptions. A wandering spiritualist about whose magical powers and integrity local accounts vary. Aravindan here illustrates the tentativeness of all human estimations and projections and the mystery that surrounds the final truth about an individual. The film interweaves the many stories about Esthappan into a complex narrative structure, avoiding crystallisations and keeping the mystery of the man intact.

Documentaries

He is currently making a documentary on breast feeding sponsored by the Kerala government and CARE, using his own paintings along with those of others. It is in colour and expected to be of 10 minutes' duration.

Also involved in a series of instructional films on all aspects of rubber production. It is for the Rubber Board and meant to be shown to the plantation workers.

Currently (mid-1981) working on a new film *Pokkuveyil* (Twilight). The film traces major events in a young man's life; his introspective nature, his alienation from his girl friend, his brief interaction with a political extremist, and his subsequent breakdown.

Still from Pokkuveyil (Twilight).

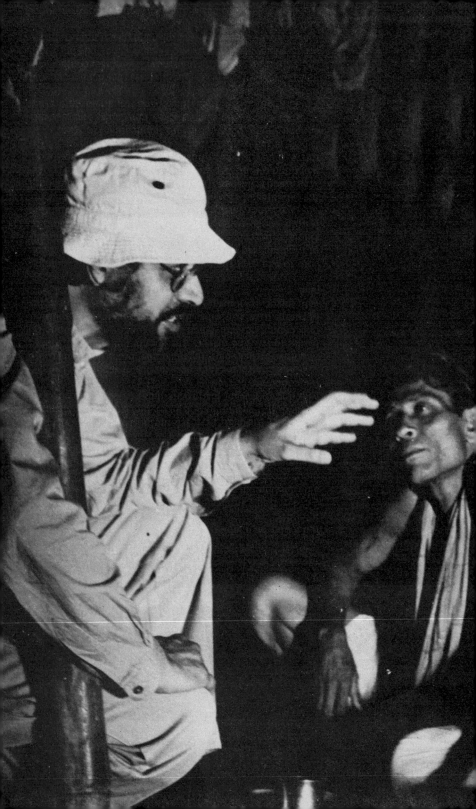

SHYAM BENEGAL

Shyam Benegal shot to fame so fast with his very first film that people forget the long training and hard struggle preceding it. He made his first feature *Ankur* (The Seedling) when he was 38. He had been ready to make the film twelve years earlier. He found an unexpected backer in 'Blaze', an advertising-distribution company. Another year went by in shunting across the country, as three leading stars turned down the central role, because it was "unglamorous."

Benegal says, "When I was so badly stuck in *Ankur* because I was literally banking on star quality, I decided never to fall into that trap. New actors may exact more time and effort but they don't hold a director to ransom as stars can do in our country." The Benegal repertory of actors is now so highly regarded that the top stars vie to act for him — on his terms.

Land up unannounced at Shyam Benegal's flat in Peddar Road (a densely populated area of Bombay) and if he and his wife Nira are at home, it is likely that they will be listening to recorded music. Both are avid concert-goers, and have eclectic tastes in music. Favourites include the Jaipur school of Hindustani music, Mozart and jazz.

The Benegals keep an open house and are known for their gregariousness and Nira's superb cooking. Frequent visitors include a close-knit group of friends — Satyadev Dubey who writes, acts and produces plays, Girish Karnad also a playwright, Govind Nihalani a cameraman, Jennifer and Shashi Kapoor both of whom act in films. All of them are involved in some way with Shyam's films. Nihalani, Karnad and Dubey are also film makers in their own right and Kapoor a producer, but when it is a question of working for a film of Shyam's, they quite willingly drop everything else and get involved in his latest project. If any of this group are present when you go visiting you will enter in the midst of a loud and intense discussion on topics ranging from films to politics to gourmet cooking.

The camaraderie and informality of "doing things with a group of friends" carries over into Shyam's film making as well. While he is intense and concentrates totally on a particular shot or scene, immediately it is over he can indulge with great gusto in horseplay and telling smutty jokes. If the film in question is being shot outside Bombay, afterwork hours become a voyage of discovery. The film unit, led by Shyam and Govind, scour the countryside for the specialities of the local cuisine, headgear, footwear, clothing, handicrafts and what-have-you. The folk music of the area is taped to add to Shyam's large music collection.

Besides making feature films, Shyam also makes advertising shorts and documentaries. His office, a rabbit warren of cubicles, situated about ten minutes away from his flat, is always buzzing with activity. He seems to be doing ten things at one time, dictating a letter, listening to a script for a possible feature, talking on the phone, discussing the layout for a poster or the details of an ad-film, and putting up with an unending stream of visitors. Many of the younger film makers come to Shyam with their problems as he is a Director of the National Film Development Corporation and the President of the Society which runs the Film Institute in Pune. When the going gets too rough, Nira lands up with a rescue operation and insists that Shyam go home and take some rest and No Visitors Allowed.

Shyam comes from a large family. He is one of ten children, and so is quite used to working amidst noise and crowds without losing concentration. His father, a professional photographer, also kept an open house and revelled in having a stream of visitors who would argue and debate the vital issues of that era.

The place was Hyderabad. The Period: the forties and fifties. Shyam was fortunate in growing up in an atmosphere which allowed a cross-current of various influences. His father came from an orthodox brahmin family, but was himself an agnostic who would not allow any ritual to be conducted in the house. He was a Gandhian nationalist; one of Shyam's brothers who lives in Calcutta was a communist sympathiser, another brother was for a time a member of the revivalist Hindu nationalist faction, the RSS.

The family were originally from South Kanara in Karnataka and speak an unwritten west-coast dialect, Konkani. The State language in Hyderabad was Urdu, spoken by the ruling Muslim aristocracy. But the language of the common people is Telugu. Shyam knows both languages but is more fluent in Konkani and English. At one time he even wrote short stories and poems in English. Some were published in American and Indian journals.

The neighbourhood where Shyam grew up was in Alwal, a semi-rural settlement ten miles outside the city. Most of the neighbours were connected in some way with a small ancient temple nearby which had an enormous wooden chariot taken out in an annual procession. Others owned fields, which were farmed by hired labour while they themselves held down jobs in the city. This semi-rural background was one of the most deeply felt influences, and forms the backdrop and subject matter of his first two films.

At that time the feudal State of Hyderabad, vassal to the British crown, was ruled by an eccentric and auto-cratic ruler whose doings added to the peculiar charm of the city, a mixture of whimsicality and perverseness. Shyam is planning another film, set in the exact suburban feudal milieu in which he grew up. Appropriately, perhaps, it is to be a comedy set in the forties.

One of the most violent events in recent Indian history was the Communist backed peasant uprising in Telengana which took place in the villages around Hyderabad in 1948 when Shyam was at a very impressionable age. Many young men from Hyderabad left their studies to take part in the uprising. The peasant revolt was crushed by the Indian army. The Prime Minister, Jawaharlal Nehru, offered an amnesty to all the young students who took part and many resumed their studies. A group of these Telengana activists, older than Shyam by some years, were his classmates and they created a lasting impression. His knowledge of Marxism and the Left movement all over the world dates from this period. He can talk with remarkable felicity and in great detail on its varied aspects, Zapata and the Mexican Revolution, the American Wobblies, the develop-ment of the thoughts of Mao, Franz Fanon, or the history of the Communist Party of India. When he was a student of Economics at Osmania University a Dutch vedantist introduced Shyam to Existentialism.

Having made his first home movie at the age of 12 with his father's hand-cranked camera, films were an abiding passion. He founded one of Hyderabad's first film societies and was an enthusiastic and active member. Theatre was also an area which interested him. The Inter-University Youth Festivals were a big event in those days and Shyam led the Osmania contingent two or three times to Delhi. One of these visits proved decisive. Jawaharlal Nehru gave a speech on the subliminal influence that the mass media could exert. This concept interested Shyam greatly.

Soon afterwards a friend in Bombay promised to get him a job in a Bombay advertising firm. Shyam chucked up everything and bought a oneway ticket to Bombay with just five rupees in his pocket. The promised job never materialised. But he finally got an opening in Lintas, a prestigious agency, as a copywriter. In Lintas he worked his way up to scripting ad-films, then supervising them, and finally being allowed to make them himself. In between he collaborated on the screenplay of the famous Malayalam novel 'Chemeen' to be made by Shyam's cousin, film maker Guru Dutt. The film was never made but Shyam was then able to script another film which became *Ankur* ten years later. In these ten years he made more than 250 advertisement shorts and about 30 documentaries.

In 1979 Shyam was a recipient of the Bhabha Fellowship, an annual grant given to select artists. Part of the project he took up involved working in the United States as an associate television producer. After the Bhabha Fellowship, he set out as an independent producer of advertising shorts and documentaries. And in 1973, when his daughter Pia was eight years old, Shyam completed his first feature film *Ankur*.

Perhaps the most controversial aspect of Shyam's films is his depiction of women. The traditionalists feel his approach is too "un-Indian" and one well-known film producer asked that his films be banned on that score. On the other hand, feminists feel he only shows women as "victims." The truth is somewhere in between. No other Indian film maker though has shown as much sympathy with the female characters he has depicted. This, Shyam feels, is due to the influence of his father and his wife.

Unlike most men of his class, Shyam's father was much more particular about the education of his daughters than his sons, who he felt could fend for themselves. Shyam's wife Nira Mukerji comes from a family of strong, independent women and a milieu entirely the opposite of Shyam's: an urbanised, sophisticated, North-Indian Christian background. She works as an editor in one of the leading publishing houses in Bombay.

There are two things which Shyam can talk about at great length — a car and good food but he can neither cook nor drive and leaves both to Nira. He is allowed to cheer from the sidelines though. Sometimes one has to take a back seat!

Shama Zaidi

Benegal wraps all his messages in a ravishing flow of movement and images. His direction carries a personal stamp which is sufficiently strong to be recognisable without harming the overall story.

Derek Elley
Films and Filming (U.K.)
May 1976

MANTHAN
(The Churning)

The Untouchables in line to sell their milk collection: Bhola (centre) becomes their rebel leader.

1976/Col/134 mins/Hindi
Direction
Shyam Benegal
Screenplay
Vijay Tendulkar
Camera
Govind Nihalani
Music
Vanraj Bhatia
Art Direction
Shama Zaidi
Editing
Bhanudas
Players
Girish Karnad (Dr. Rao),
Mohan Agashe (Deshmukh),
Anant Nag (Chandavarkar),
Smita Patil (Bindu),
Yashpal (Bindu's husband),
Naseeruddin Shah (Bhola),
Anjali Paigankar (Harijan girl),
Amrish Puri (Mishraji),
Kulbhushan Kharbanda
(village headman),
Abha Dhulia (Dr. Rao's wife
Shanta).
Enquiries
Gujarat Cooperative Milk
Marketing Federation,
Anand,
Kaira District,
Gujarat.

Manthan is an unusual film in that it was financed by the the farmers of Gujarat State themselves, who through their milk cooperatives, donated two rupees each—500,000 of them! This amount more than paid for the production of the film. Benegal chose to make a film about the farmers themselves and their problems.

Manthan concerns a government official, Dr. Rao, a veterinarian, who is sent from Bombay with a small team of helpers to set up a milk cooperative in a little village in Gujarat State. These strangers from the city quickly run foul of the local dairy produce contractor, Mishraji, who has been underpaying local farmers for their milk for years.

Dr. Rao tries to enlist the help of the exploited Untouchable community. Gradually his policy begins to work. He risks attending to an Untouchable's seriously ill child. He gives an injection and the child is cured. The Untouchables are impressed and come flocking to him. The hostile contractor, though, causes trouble which is exacerbated when Chandavarkar, the cooperative worker, has an affair with an Untouchable girl, which sparks off village animosities and rivalries. A demonstration meeting held by the cooperative's team is stoned. Chandavarkar is summarily sacked for his affair with the Untouchable girl, who is whipped and chained for her indiscretion.

Dr. Rao is an urban Westernised Indian who wants to serve as a catalyst to change but is held back by an in-built patronising attitude. He meets a smouldering, sullen village wife, Bindu, and is strongly attracted to her. He hides his feelings behind a moral commitment although the real reason could be an awareness of his superiority. A subtle connection is conveyed between his political and sexual life. Both contain degrees of repression, reflecting an inability on his part to be really involved in either.

Dr. Rao's ambivalence contrasts sharply to that of his aide, Deshmukh, who is pragmatic enough to advise keeping aloof from village politics and sensibilities. The local headman, referred to as *Sarpanch,* is also at cross-purposes. He had asked the government to set up the cooperative mainly to be able to make it his power base as its Chairman. Instead, he loses the post to an Untouchable rival, Moti. The humiliation drives him to befriend Mishraji, who does not want his private dairy to be endangered by the cooperative.

The contractor then uses tactics of sabotage. The co-operative's trucks carrying milkcans "break down" en route to the town. The drivers are openly defiant. The soured milk cannot be sold. When Dr. Rao uncovers the duplicity, Mishraji tries to bribe him, an offer that is spurned with anger, revitalising the despairing Rao to enforce his plan.

Dr. Rao realises that he needs the help of an insider, both to win over the majority and to combat the cunning of Mishraji. He picks a natural leader from among them, Bhola, a fiercely sensitive Untouchable. Bhola is initially hostile because he suspects all outsiders as exploiters. His own father, an urban contractor, abandoned his mother for the lures of city life.

Bindu's husband is an idler who lives off her hard work and resents her growing involvement with the coope-rative. The suspicious husband has her buffalo poisoned. Bindu is left without her sole means of support and is conned by the contractor into implicating Dr. Rao.

Dr. Rao's wife Shanta joins him later. She is a city woman, bored by the village and totally disinterested in her husband's efforts to bring change and prosperity into the lives of the poor. Shanta feels that being educated she is different and better than the villagers. Her contact with urban society is her transistor which keeps playing Hindi film songs. She questions her husband on her importance to him as opposed to the village.

Inevitably, the caste and hierarchical confrontations come to a head. The Untouchables' huts are set on fire. The private contractor uses the opportunity to buy back the homeless villagers' loyalty by giving them gifts and money. The opportunistic charity dupes the naive villagers. It all seems to be reverting back to square one. Mishraji triumphantly uses political pull to have the cooperative organisers recalled. The dejected team disband and leave. There is, unknown to them, a ray of hope: Bhola. He tries to revive the cooperative with the help of Moti. But their enemies are still there.

Benegal says: "The problems of caste have reached a point of decay where it is used to oppress people, but it cannot be wished away by legislation. It can only be changed by confrontation between castes. *Manthan* suggests a call to change via such a confrontation. In the end, a chord has been struck."

The film is told with a firm narrative grasp, superb photography (Benegal's films look better than any other Indian film), fine ensemble acting, and is full of magical little moments such as one where the hero, lonely for his wife, eyes a lovely village girl as she draws water from the well. Shyam Benegal has emerged as one of India's most important directors, and this is a fine introduction to his work.

1978 Sydney Film Festival brochure

BHUMIKA
(The Role)

1977/Col/142 mins/Hindi
Direction
Shyam Benegal
Screenplay
Girish Karnad.
Satyadev Dubey,
Shyam Benegal
Camera
Govind Nihalani
Music
Vanraj Bhatia
Art Direction
Shama Zaidi
Editing
Bhanudas
Players
Smita Patil (Usha),
Anant Nag (Rajan),
Amrish Puri (Vinayak Kale),
Naseeruddin Shah
(Sunil Verma),
Sulabha Deshpande
(Shantabai),
Kulbhushan Kharbanda
(Harilal),
B. V. Karanth (the father),
Baby Ruksana (Usha as a child),
Amol Palekar (Keshav Dalvi).
Enquiries
Blaze Film Enterprises,
Lalji Naranu
Memorial Bldg.,
Churchgate, Bombay 400 020.
Tel: 298257/298696

The film star reacts to accusations flung at her by her family.

Bhumika is the story of Usha, whose screen name is Urvashi. She is a famous film star and singer. The Period: late thirties.

As a child, Usha lives a fettered, fitful existence with her grumpy mother, her long-suffering grandmother (who was denied marriage: being a courtesan musician, she could only be a kept woman in her time), and an alcoholic father. A family friend and benefactor is Keshav (also the mother's lover) who takes more than a fatherly interest in the spirited child. Usha's only escape from her overbearing world is her lonely flights into the woods — and her love and aptitude for singing, taught to her by her kindly grandmother, a noted singer herself.

Usha is beset by adult woes and frustrations. Her parents quarrel constantly. Her mother resents her music lessons, her sense of independence, and perhaps, Keshav's watchful eye.

Bhumika is
**based on the biography of
Hansa Wadkar, a star of
the Marathi folk theatre
and cinema of the forties.
In a way she was the Joan
Crawford of the Marathi
scene, getting through men
by the dozen and bottles
by the thousand ... What
Benegal has done is to paint
a magnificent visual
recreation of those
extraordinary days, and
one that is also sensitive to
the agonies and
predicament of a talented
woman whose need for
security was only matched
by her insistence on
freedom.**

Derek Malcolm
1978 London Film festival
brochure

When Usha's father dies, Keshav steps in as head of the household. He notes Usha's talent as a singer and brings the family to Bombay hoping that Usha's singing will help her get a break in films. She is selected at her very first audition.

Usha rises fast in the film world. Her leading co-star is Rajan, handsome and self-centred, not yet ready to commit himself. In defiance (more of her mother) Usha marries Keshav. She decides also to quit acting. But Keshav, a steady loser in business, forces her to continue. The entire family depends on her earnings.

Life at home is stifling for Usha. Though she has a daughter, Sushma, she has no respect for her weak, jealous and grasping husband, or her resentful, grudging mother. Her adored grandmother has died.

The unreality, romanticism and synthetic glamour of her screen life and her undefined needs and frustrations as a woman make her very susceptible. Her restlessness becomes acute. She runs to Rajan, who does not want to become a scapegoat in her scramble for happiness. He prefers to remain her friend.

A dashing young director enters her life, Sunil Verma, given to airy intellectual talk. When she becomes pregnant, her husband accuses her of adultery, and forces her to have an abortion. Sunil and Usha enter into a melodramatic suicide pact, following a night of passion. It doesn't work because the two dupe each other.

Usha cuts herself off totally from her husband. She meets a curt, elderly man, Kale, who is staying in the same hotel. She is impressed with his sense of authority. He is wealthy and takes her to his feudal estate. Although his mistress, she is given the rights of a wife: full run of the house, his son's affection, and respect from his neglected, paralysed wife. Usha realises she is virtually a prisoner. True to tradition, she cannot be seen outside the mansion. She secretly writes to her husband, who arrives with the police to rescue her.

She returns to Bombay, to her hotel, now a wiser, older woman. Her daughter offers her a home, having married and settled (to Usha's relief). Usha declines the offer. She turns down Keshav's request to give them both another chance. Rajan telephones, sounding more insistent, but she does not answer. She decides to face her future, alone.

The director has re-created the period of the thirties, forties and fifties with snippets from various genres of films that were popular at that time, through right atmospheric visuals and sound effects. He presents a working woman who struggled through a profession which was both patronised and looked down upon by society. He has chosen for his film an interesting individual, an actress, and reveals the pain and the turmoil she experiences as she moves further away from her simple life to the unavoidable and, indeed, necessary glamour and loneliness of stardom.

Filmography

1974

ANKUR (The Seedling)
Col/181 mins/Hindi
Lead players: Shabana Azmi, Anant Nag, Sadhu Meher, Priya Tendulkar.

Benegal's first film is based on the story he wrote when he was 16. It is set in the feudal society of South India and manifests the director's humanitarian concern for the dispossessed. An unwittingly arrogant young man — still a student — is sent by his father to manage their farm land. He seduces his attractive maid servant, both out of boredom and sexual frustration. The arrival of his wife, the servant's pregnancy and the fear of discovery lead to a violent climax, when the deaf-mute husband of the servant is mercilessly beaten. Feudalism implies ownership of people.

1975

NISHANT (Night's End)
Col/140 mins/Hindi
Lead players: Shabana Azmi, Girish Karnad, Smita Patil, Amrish Puri, Mohan Agashe, Naseeruddin Shah

The seed of violence explicit in the final scene of *Ankur*, where a young boy throws a stone at the landlord's house, is carried to fruition in the second film by Benegal, again set in the same feudal milieu. The arrival of an idealistic schoolmaster in the village sets off a chain reaction. His wife is kidnapped by the powerful landowning family. She becomes the mistress of the youngest brother who is in love with her. The police do not help and the hitherto docile schoolmaster leads the peasants to revolt. Benegal uses the metaphor of woman's sexual exploitation to stand for the entire process of class antagonism and oppression.

CHARANDAS CHOR (Charandas the Thief)
B&W/112 mins/Hindi
Lead players: Lalu Ram, Sadhu Meher, Smita Patil, Anjali Paigankar, Habib Tanvir

A story about a legendary thief who takes a vow never to lie and then makes impossible pledges for which he pays with his life. He becomes a hero, the great outlaw of his time and the benefactor of the poor. The film treats the story as a slapstick comedy. Produced by the Children's Film Society, India

1976 ### MANTHAN (The Churning)
1977 ### BHUMIKA (The Role)
KONDURA/ANUGRAHAM (The Boon)
Col/125 mins Hindi/118 mins Telugu
Lead players: Anant Nag, Vanisree, Smita Patil

The film is a psychological and philosophical exploration of the repercussions created by the granting of a supernatural boon. Parsuram, the newly married brahmin, is granted a root that induces abortion. Strict celibacy is enjoined upon him. The complex course of events reaches a tragic denouement brought about by the interaction of Parsuram's own doubts, his visions of the goddess who uncannily resembles his wife, the devious schemes of the inscrutable landlord and his problematic family. A subjective thread of sexual obsession runs through the film.

1978 JUNOON (The Obsession)
Col/141 mins/Hindi
Lead Players: Shashi Kapoor, Jennifer Kendal,
Shabana Azmi, Nafisa Ali, Naseeruddin Shah,
Kulbhushan Kharbanda.
Benegal turns to the turbulent period of 1857, when the Indian soldiers of the East India Company's regiments mutinied against the British. It forms a violent background to a muted, inter-racial love story between a young English girl and a Pathan (Muslim) nobleman. The human story is interlinked with the fortunes of the war. The film is based on a short story, 'The Flight of Pigeons' which in turn, is inspired by the memoirs of an English woman, a survivor of the Mutiny.

1981 KALYUG (The Machine Age)
Col/154 mins/Hindi
Lead players: Shashi Kapoor, Rekha, Anant Nag, Victor Banerjee, Supriya Pathak, Kulbhushan Kharbanda, Raj Babbar
This is perhaps Benegal's most ambitious venture, inspired by the ancient Hindu epic, the 'Mahabharata'. Two powerful industrial families, first cousins and rivals in business, are irrevocably bent on a path of mutual destruction. The modern parable set in the sophisticated, urban elite of industrial India has well defined characters based on the epic archetypes. Alienation and destruction are the inevitable result of the fratricidal rivalry and corroding jealousy.

HARI HONDAL BARGADAR (Share Cropper)
tentative title. (Under production)
Col/Hindi
Lead players: Om Puri, Victor Banerjee, Gita Sen,
Rajen Tarafdar, Pankaj Kapoor, Shekhar Chatterjee,
Noni Ganguly, Sreela Majumdar
About a share cropper evicted from his small piece of land by his landlord in the very face of Land Reform Laws that are passed by the government to prevent this from happening. The film examines the implementation of land laws and attitudes of the judiciary and executive. Set as a saga, it explores a changing political climate in the life of a marginal farmer and his family.

SOME IMPORTANT DOCUMENTARIES
A Child of the Streets (1967), Close to Nature (1968), Indian Youth — an exploration (1968), Horoscope for a Child (1970), Pulsating Giant (1971), Tala and Rhythm (1972), The Shruti and Graces of Indian Music (1972), The Raag Yaman Kalyan (1972), Notes on a Green Revolution (1972), Learning Modules for Rural Children (1974/75), A Quiet Revolution (1975), New Horizons in Steel (1977).

BASU CHATTERJI

Basu Chatterji, known for
the keenness of his sense
of observation, translates
with great feeling the
tensions and the conflicts
of a situation which moves
to life the great majority
of the Indians.

Henri Micciollo
Cinema Magazine (France)
April 1978

Basu Chatterji is, without doubt, India's most prolific and speedy film director. A late beginner, he has so far established an average of three films a year, made at lightning speed, each within a span of about forty shooting shifts. Obviously, he does not believe in the long haul of sporadic shootings. Built into his thinking are several vital factors that give shape and energy to his work. True to his motto— speed is of the essence — he practises an economy of time invariably allowing an economy of budget. In truth, Basu Chatterji is now the master of the low budget feature film. The commercial and popular success of his early work has won him a captive audience for his later films.

An interesting part of his creative work is his control of the screenplay. In all his films, without exception, right from *Sara Akash* (The Whole Sky) in 1969 to *Man Pasand* (To One's Liking) in 1979, he has meticulously registered every word, every idea on paper, paying detailed attention to dialogue and patterns of movement. A Basu Chatterji screenplay, if examined, clearly reveals the amount of thought and paperwork involved in each scene. It's all there from the pin to the elephant.

Working for 'Blitz', the popular leftist weekly, for 19 years as a cartoonist, he bided his time, watching, waiting, absorbing. His sense of observation, particularly in the realm of action and reaction, helped him store these molecules of reality quite unconsciously over the years. Now, pouring out of his pen and onto celluloid are small touches of pathos, humour and a sharp yank of the heartstrings, all terribly familiar and close to human experience. It is said that he has made an art of the "dailiness" of life. Perhaps we harried humans fail to see beauty in the ritual of daily routine. He calls his work an easy-flowing reconstruction of human observation.

A film society worker since 1959, Basu Chatterji had ample opportunity to see the best of world cinema. Slowly, observing became learning. In 1968, as assistant director on *Teesri Kasam* (Third Oath), produced by the late Shailendra, a noted lyricist, he learnt his craft. "I did everything there was to be done on the set. No work was uninteresting or below me. I had to catch up." He caught up with his first film *Sara Akash* (The Whole Sky), a low budget venture which immediately won him recognition. The Big Bad Wolf of commercialism is no nightmare to Basu Chatterji. He believes in its existence and works within its framework. "But the film has to be creatively satisfying within the framework. I cannot compromise there. A fusion of Art and Commerce is best, and one struggles to achieve this, whatever the pitfalls," he says.

It is whispered among new actors struggling for a break that to meet Basu Chatterji is not very difficult. He is open to new faces, new ideas and he scans carefully the city's theatre and television media for fresh talent.

And indeed he takes amazing risks with newcomers, relying mainly on his instinct for a face, a figure, a sense of timing. He has seldom been proved wrong.

His approach is casual and there is virtually no tension in the atmosphere around his location. Approachable, he listens quietly to suggestions from his actors, often stuffing a large white handkerchief into his mouth, and gazing in the opposite direction. Often the suggestion is accepted, even incorporated into the work. Built like a truck driver, gentle as a lamb, he prefers to brief his actors with hints and examples rather than heavy-handed direction. It is a touch so feather-light that you often don't know it's there. Rather like capturing gossamer.

His film themes have often been the subject of much controversy. In the India of 1981, the socially committed film is very much in vogue. Perhaps critics have found it puzzling that a major talent such as Basu Chatterji's has concerned itself with beds of roses and dappled sunshine. His reply is simple. "Well, that's the way I accept life. Yes, I know there's sorrow and misery in this world. I'm part of it. I sense its reality. But still, there are moments of beauty too, of pleasure. I feel, why not capture that essence, and deal with it. Lots of directors deal with suspense, sorrow, morbidity. It makes for variety. My personal philosophy is that life is not full of messages. There are simple elements that give us great happiness. That's what I like to project. The small joys of living." For the most part, he has clung to this professed philosophy, but a deeper probing of the man and his work reveals a somewhat different picture. Patterns for the future are in the slow process of change, and as seen through a kaleidoscope, Basu Chatterji's focus may be elsewhere. One sees him at a crossroad.

Pearl Padamsee

In one decade, the seventies, Basu Chatterji made over twenty films. In three years, '76 to '79, he made a dozen comedies. Yet, his first film was a serious, finely etched study of domestic disharmony caused by an early, unwanted marriage. Many a year and comedy later, Chatterji reverted to being serious once again in a recent film called *Jeena Yahan* (Living Here), which examines city life, its social disparities and the ugliness of outmoded village traditions.

There is ample proof that Chatterji's talent covers a wide canvas. But his forte has been in dealing with the comedy of manners in a contemporary, more urbanised and familiar setting. His contribution in making us laugh at ourselves is almost unique when seen against the escapist extravaganzas of commercial cinema or the sombre introspection of the "other" cinema.

Most big stars are happy to work for him, and his films feature possibly the widest range among them for any one director.

SARA AKASH
(The Whole Sky)

The wedding night: the nervous, resentful bridegroom and his unsuspecting bride.

1969/B&W/100 mins/Hindi
Direction/Screenplay
Basu Chatterji
Camera
K. K. Mahajan
Music
Salil Chowdhury
Editing
G. G. Mayekar
Players
Rakesh Pandey (Samar, the bridegroom), Madhu Chanda (Prabha, the bride), A. K. Hangal (the father), Dina Pathak (the mother), Mani Kaul (the elder brother), Tarla Mehta (the elder daughter-in-law), Nandita Thakur (the younger sister-in-law), Jalal Agha (the college friend).
Enquiries
Cineye Films, Arvind Chambers, 3rd floor, 194 Adarsh-Kurla Road, Andheri East, Bombay 400 069. Tel: 534522

The film is set in a traditional joint family household, where the father is in authority and the eldest daughter-in-law rules the hearth under her mother-in-law's surveillance. It is the elders who decide when a son is to be married and they select the bride. Early marriage is the rule. A major consideration in the choice is the amount of dowry the girl brings with her. The new bride is expected to automatically fit into her slot, sharing the burden of household work and not speaking unless spoken to. Personal relations between husband and wife are, to a considerable extent, controlled by the exigencies of the household.

Samar, the hero of the film, is a young university student who has marriage foisted on him very much against his wishes. His sister-in-law is pregnant, and the bride is needed to help with the household. The considerable dowry is another attraction. So his protests are overruled. The bride, Prabha, is a college graduate — unusual for a tradition-bound North Indian family.

From the start, the marriage runs into heavy weather. Samar's resistance to the marriage is compounded by his almost pathological shyness and manifests itself in an attitude of hostility towards Prabha. The wedding night, fraught with the tension of not knowing what to do, is a fiasco, as Samar stalks out to sleep on the terrace.

The reaction of the family is predictable. Samar at first is chided for his unreasonable aversion to his wife,

One of the most accessible of the "new" films, *Sara Akash* has also enjoyed (in India) a relative commercial success. Adapted from a well-known novel it takes a sensitive look at the problems faced by two newly-weds.

National Film Theatre (U.K.) brochure
Season of New Indian Films
December 1972

but soon left alone. Prabha has to suffer the discipline of the domestic routine that is heavy-handedly imposed on her, both to show her her place and as subtle admonition for failing to please her husband. The elder daughter-in-law envies Prabha her youth, good looks, and most of all, her education. She loses no opportunity to confound matters between the young couple and to isolate and ridicule the girl; for example, she over-salts the first meal cooked by the new wife. The only sympathy Prabha gets is from Samar's sister, who has been abandoned by an unfaithful husband.

When the elder daughter-in-law has her baby, the work of the entire household falls on the new bride. She finds it difficult to cope and is repeatedly insulted. The final straw is when she unwittingly uses holy clay to clean utensils. Samar uses this occasion to slap her in front of the household, making her humiliation complete.

At the younger sister-in-law's suggestion, Prabha leaves for a four-month stay with her parents. Her husband misses her once she is gone and has romantic daydreams about their reconciliation. On her return, the family is gratified to learn that she has not mentioned her plight to her parents. However, neither husband nor wife can break the ice and Prabha goes about her chores in defiant silence. This time it is she who decides to sleep elsewhere. As the lonely and miserable girl weeps audibly on the terrace, Samar approaches her to ask the reason. The unprotesting silence with which she has borne her humiliation at last gives way to anger. The husband is finally able to express his genuine remorse and the film closes with the hint of a marriage finally consummated.

Amitabha Mukherjee

Filmography

1969   **SARA AKASH (The Whole Sky)**

1971   **PIYA KA GHAR (House of the Beloved)**
Col/142 mins/Hindi
Lead Players: Jaya Bhaduri, Anil Dhawan
Basu Chatterji's second film shifts the scene to Bombay, commenting on the acute housing problem in gently humorous and human terms.

1973   **US PAAR (Across the River)**
Col/125 mins/Hindi
Lead Players: Vinod Mehra, Moushumi Chatterjee, Padma Khanna
A tempestuous love story of a college boy from a small town and a gypsy girl working in a fair.

1974   **RAJNIGANDHA (Tuberoses)**
Col/110 mins/Hindi
Lead Players: Amol Palekar, Vidya Sinha, Dinesh Thakur
Deepa, a research student in Delhi, comes to Bombay for an interview and meets an old boyfriend, a firebrand

student leader turned suave ad-man. Pining for her is Sandip, lovable, cheeky and annoyingly absentminded. She settles for the old faithful.

1975 **CHOTI SI BAAT (A Trifle)**
Col/120 mins/Hindi
Lead Players: Amol Palekar, Vidya Sinha
A timid young man follows a lively working girl to and fro from her office. A potential rival sends him scurrying to an expert for a crash course in courtship. It works.

1976 **CHIT-CHOR (He Stole My Heart)**
Col/104 mins/Hindi
Lead Players: Amol Palekar, Zarina Wahab,
Vijayendra Ghatge
A comedy of mistaken identity about a village school master with a marriageable daughter, an eligible engineer, and an undesirable rival. True love wins in the end.

1977 **SWAMI (The Saint)**
Col/130 mins/Hindi
Lead Players: Shabana Azmi, Girish Karnad
Saudamini, a self-willed girl, is forced to marry an introvert widower who lives in a joint family. Gradually, she comes to admire her husband's generosity, and tolerance in offering her the freedom to go back to her first love.

SAFED JHOOT (The White Lie)
Col/129 mins/Hindi
Lead Players: Ashok Kumar, Vinod Mehra,
Mithu Mukherjee
A comedy highlighting the troubles of a newly married young man unable to get leave from his tough boss.

PRIYATAMA (The Beloved)
Col/140 mins/Hindi
Lead Players: Jeetendra, Neetu Singh, Utpal Dutt
A lighthearted look at the house-keeping problems of a TV producer and the pampered daughter of a rich judge.

KHATTA MEETHA (Sweet and Sour)
Col/134 mins/Hindi
Lead Players: Ashok Kumar, Pearl Padamsee
A middle-aged widow and widower, with their separate broods of highly individualistic children, get married and *all* of them live together happily ever after.

1978 **CHAKRAVYUHA (The Labyrinth)**
Col/137 mins/Hindi
Lead Players: Rajesh Khanna, Neetu Singh
Inspired by *39 Steps,* the film takes the hero on a frenetic train journey; a journalist who has essential information and his girlfriend are implicated.

DILLAGI (Mischief)
Col/122 mins/Hindi
Lead Players: Dharmendra, Hema Malini
A handsome young lecturer, with a penchant for erotic Sanskrit poetry, working in a women's college stirs up his students, including a stern chemistry lecturer.

TUMHARE LIYE (For Your Sake)
Col/134 mins/Hindi
Lead Players: Ashok Kumar, Sanjeev Kumar, Vidya Sinha
A woman is haunted by a curse: she will die when she gives birth to her first child. The curse is circumvented in the second birth.

DO LADKE DONO KADKE (Two Bankrupt Boys)
Col/125 mins/Hindi
Lead Players: Amol Palekar, Asrani, Moushumi Chatterji
A hilarious story of two petty, bumbling crooks who unwittingly kidnap a young boy for ransom. With big time professionals and police chasing them, they turn into saviours. The disapproving sister of one of them relents and marries the brother's friend.

1979 ### MANZIL (The Destination)
Col/121 mins/Hindi
Lead Players: Amitabh Bachchan, Moushumi Chatterjee
A very ambitious but poor young man meets a rich girl. The first inadvertent lie leads to a maze of lies. He finally gets the girl because of his sincerity. A comedy tinged with pathos.

JEENA YAHAN (Living Here)
Col/105 mins/Hindi
Lead Players: Shabana Azmi, Shekhar Kapoor
Basu Chatterji returns to the serious theme of urban living. A young couple get married almost casually, happy in their jobs and their circle of friends. The young woman visits her in-laws in a small town for reasons of health. The euphoria is soon dispelled by the narrow minded and high-handed behaviour of her mother-in-law. She comes back to Bombay freeing her young sister-in-law from an awful marriage to an old man.

BATON BATON MEIN (A Casual Affair)
Col/122 mins/Hindi
Lead Players: Amol Palekar, Tina Munim, Pearl Padamsee
Romance is the outcome of proximity while commuting to work. The young couple live in a Bombay suburb that is predominantly Roman Catholic. The young man is willing to woo but unwilling to marry. The over-eager mother of the girl and his own domineering mother pull him in opposite directions. All ends well with a group photo of the two families at the church.

PREM VIVAH (Love Marriage)
Col/140 mins/Hindi
Lead Players: Utpal Dutt, Asha Parekh,
Bindiya Goswami and Mithun Chakraborty
A quadrangular love story. A young engaged couple is desperate to find a mature groom for the exacting older sister. The psychiatrist and TV personality they locate is eminently suitable but he falls for the matchmaking younger sister!

1979   RATNADEEP (The Jewelled Lamp)
Col/131 mins/Hindi
Lead Players: Girish Karnad, Hema Malini and A. K. Hangal
A fictionalised account of an alleged real-life incident
that rocked Bengal in the 1920s. A look-alike imposter is
welcomed to the ancestral home of a rich, land-owning
family as the long-lost husband of the beautiful woman.
The man falls in love with her. Prompted by an uneasy
conscience, he confesses that he had found the diary of
the dead man. The woman dies of shock.

1980   MAN PASAND (To One's Liking)
Col/135 mins/Hindi
Lead Players: Dev Anand, Girish Karnad and Tina Munim
This is an Indianised version of *My Fair Lady*. The
social aspirant is a seller of twigs (the indigenous toothbrush)
and she wants to be a singer. The debonair professor is a
musician.

APNE PARAYE (Our Relations)
Col/130 mins/Hindi
Lead Players: Shabana Azmi, Amol Palekar, Girish Karnad
A story of the bonds and frustrations of a traditional joint
family living in Calcutta. A lovable idler, a cousin of the
two brothers, both professionals, lives with the family.
His efficient wife manages the household accounts and the
kitchen. They are humiliated and forced to leave by one
of the jealous women, and go to their ancestral village
home. Finally they are all reconciled.

Currently working on:
HAMARI BAHU ALKA (Our daughter-in-law)
The comic plight of a young man forced to concentrate
on his studies and denied the company of his new bride
by his father. The father is rich but uneducated.

SHAUKEEN (The Afficionados)
*Lead Players: Ashok Kumar, A. K. Hangal, Utpal Dutt,
Rati Agnihotri*
Promises to be a hilarious comedy of three elderly men
amorously interested in a pretty girl, the fiancee of their
chauffeur.

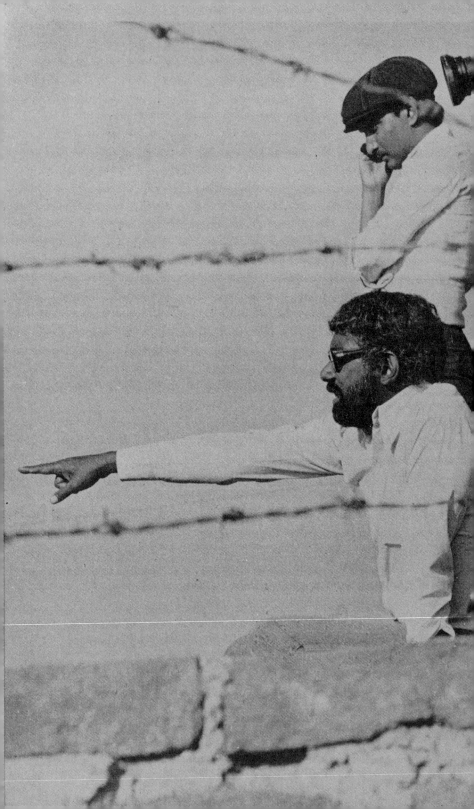

RABINDRA DHARMARAJ

If it was difficult to admire him, it was not easy either to disapprove of him. He had the right attitudes. He struck all the wrong poses. He also died young. That was probably the most unforgivable act in his short life. But that was how Rabindra Dharmaraj always was. Chaotic, disturbed and unknowingly charming. He spoke of death, achievement and failure with dispassionate eloquence.

A colleague

Rabindra Dharmaraj was only 33 years and one feature film old when he died in a Bombay hospital on February 11, 1981, following an ulcer complaint. His sudden death was seen by many as the tragic loss of a highly artistic talent, and of a warm and sensitive man.

Despite his premature death, Rabindra, or Rabin as he was called, had seen more of life than most.

The "psychedelic sixties" were a formative period in Rabin's life. Then a student of Literature and History at St. Stephen's College, Delhi, Rabin was swept up in the tumult of socio-political feeling that characterised the youth movement of that time. The drug-culture had reached the college campus. Not surprisingly, Rabin too was lured by its fascination, with the "new consciousness" with which it tempted his artistic spirit. But the passage of time did not fade its fatal attraction. He continued to indulge in drug-taking with unforeseen damage to his health and mind.

In the meantime Rabin, keenly interested in the struggling radical groups of Indian politics, had joined the vanguard of committed Marxists. The sixties' political pre-occupation with Vietnam also had a direct and profound effect on Rabin. Rejecting the easy option that his college degree had provided him occupationally, Rabin went to Vietnam as a war-correspondent. The photographs and reports he made during his two trips, 1968 and 1970, were reproduced in various international magazines and newspapers. But, inspite of this professional success, these proved trying periods for an intellect as socially and politically sensitive as Rabin's. The consciousness of his experiences in Vietnam was never to leave him entirely.

Back in India, Rabin took up a job with All India Radio in Delhi. The basic skills he learned there he developed in a formal training course in advanced film and video technique at the University of California, where he studied briefly. His love of celluloid led him into the making of numerous documentaries, various films for Bombay Television, and advertising films. His real goal was a feature, *Chakra* (The Vicious Circle), from the controversial novel by Jaywant Dalvi. Written in the early sixties, this bold and realistic portrayal of the lives of. slum dwellers won several awards for its Marathi author. The story, with its grim social comment, haunted Rabin, and he became obsessed with the idea of its production. Seven years prior to its making Rabin had already personally approached Dalvi concerning the purchase rights of the novel—although at the time he was unable even to pay for them.

Since 1973, Rabin had been working as Deputy Film Executive for Lintas India Limited, a leading advertising agency, where he had set about learning to master the medium of cinema. His enthusiasm, his originality, his compelling charm soon gave Rabin a reputation as a dynamic ad-man. From Lintas he moved to Hindustan Thompson Associates, and thence to Neo-Films as a partner in a firm making and processing advertising films. There he produced work which marked him out cinematically as a brilliant and original man, with a keen eye for visual detail, and an immaculate editing style.

But he had been writing and watching until he could shape his message with one powerful stroke. Now, with the mastery of technique that his advertising career had given him, Rabin felt ready to make his feature Chakra. This was the moment he had been waiting for with such determination and tenacity: the culmination of years in a business which, by its very nature, must have taxed his Marxist conscience fearfully. A self-contained man, Rabin's outward display of calm confidence betrayed nothing of the inner conflict he was struggling to resolve. Yet it must have burdened him.

But Rabin's Chakra was finally made in the nick of time to participate in the Panorama section of the Eighth International Film Festival of India held in New Delhi and it proved an outstanding success. A month later, Rabin was dead—sadly, before either seeing his film selected for Cannes and Locarno, or Smita Patil, his heroine, collect the National Award for the Best Actress. For us, the sadness lies in the fact that Rabin's immense artistic potential, as revealed in Chakra will now never be realised. The death of Rabin represents a loss of his personal warmth and his professional and artistic abilities which is felt deeply by friends and filmgoers alike.

Xanthe Noble

Bansi Chandragupta, the art director on Chakra, speaks of Rabin Dharmaraj's exacting eye for atmospheric detail. In fact, the most widely commended feature of the film is its authentic setting. Chandragupta says, "We tried to shoot in a real slum, but it was not possible. We needed a slum that was near a highway (to suggest that it co-existed with a teeming city life) and also near a railway track. Rabin and I kept rejecting site after site. Finally, we found an open space that was just right. It belonged to The Fertiliser Corporation of India, who very kindly agreed to let us use this vacant plot for two months. We built a brick wall there and re-created the entire slum." Indeed, the setting was so real that hawkers came daily to sell their wares. Instant roadside shops sprang up near it, including a betel-and-cigarette stall. The bulldozers razing down the slums at the end of the film are real, used by the factory to make way for its own building.

"I remember Rabin reading a poem of his. I was dazzled by the fluency and beauty of his writing. This same Rabin had the distinction of scoring a zero in one of his B.A. English papers by handing in a blank answer paper with his name and roll number neatly written on the right hand side.

"Neo-Films must have had faith in Rabin because Manmohan Shetty, a partner in the same firm, laughingly told me, 'When I first met Rabin, he wore a pair of specs with one square lens and one rectangular lens.' I never saw him like that but it must have been during his early years in Bombay when his perpetual rebellion had not taken on a constructive hue. I believe he wanted his next film to be based on Charles Sobhraj, the international criminal, involving filming all around the world. He even had the title registered: *A Man Never Dies*."

Siddharth Kak

"Rabin was in many ways an ideological buccaneer. Adventurous fact and fantasy nourished the very clear idea of the course he would chart. A complex personality, with great powers of persuasion, and also filled with, one sensed, an equal measure of disturbed anger, mostly kept in control. He spoke softly but carried many big sticks, and the culmination was *Chakra*."

Saidan Puri

"As an advertising film maker, Rabin had an advantage: his years on the agency side gave him an edge over others. Cinematically, Rabin had a rugged masculine approach. His special forte was the ability to sell his films to clients and win their total confidence. Added to which, a liquid bass voice — of which we have many a sound track on our recordings of commercials to remember him by."

Mubarak Pasricha

Rabindra Dharmaraj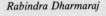

CHAKRA
(The Vicious Circle)

Amma pleads with Looka (left) not to lead her son astray.

1980/Col/140 mins/Hindi
Direction/Screenplay
Rabindra Dharmaraj
Produced by
Manmohan Shetty
Camera
Barun Mukherjee
Editing
Bhanudas
Music
Hridayanath Mangeshkar
Art Direction
Bansi Chandragupta
Players
Smita Patil (Amma),
Naseeruddin Shah (Looka),
Kulbhushan Kharbanda
(Anna), Ranjit Choudhuri
(Benwa), Anjali Paigankar
(Chenna), Uttam Sarur
(Chamanya), Savita Bajaj
(Chamanya's mother), Rohini
Hattangadi (Laxmi)
Enquiries
Neo Films, G 2 Everest
Building, Tardeo,
Bombay 400 034.
Phone: 396248

Amma is a happy, young, married woman with an infant son. Her husband murders a moneylender whom he catches attempting to rape Amma. The family flee from their village to Bombay. Soon after the husband is shot by railway guards while he is stealing tin sheets.

Years later, Amma and her son Benwa live in a hutment slum. Benwa is now a teenager. He grows up in the shadow of one of his mother's lovers, Looka, a pimp, illicit distiller, all-purpose crook who has to report to the police every month because of his previous criminal record.

The slum dwellers always welcome Looka. They like his flashy ways and they respond to his generosity and good-will, and to the way he terrorizes the neighbourhood. In the day that Looka and Benwa spend together, Benwa watches in admiration as Looka preens and whores, tells tall tales and gets drunk. Looka stays the night with Amma and tries to persuade her to let Benwa team up with him. But Amma is firm. She wants a decent life for her son without the law being at his heels or threatening his life. She also wants him to marry young and to settle down, unlike the drifting, sullied life she now leads.

Amma is delighted when Benwa decides to become a shoe-shine boy. He loses the job though because of local rivalry and bullying tactics. Others of his age try to tempt

This theme of the scavengers, the disinherited poor who are an internal time bomb in every society including our own, turned up in many films from widely scattered places ... a film from India, *Chakra,* by first-time director Rabindra Dharmaraj, treated similar material in its pitiless depiction of life among the poor in a Bombay shanty town.

Jack Kroll (on the Cannes Film Festival), Newsweek (U.S.A.) June 8, 1981

him to join the bootlegging trade.

Amma, finding Looka feckless, takes on another lover, Anna, a stolid truck driver, who offers her stability. She settles into the new hut she has always wanted with her devoted Anna; and she is with child, presumably by him. Benwa graduates into manhood with the help of Looka, who later finds a suitable bride for him, to Amma's joy. Her happiness, so suddenly within her reach, is shortlived.

Looka is stricken with syphillis, and is soon a miserable, sore-infested shell of his former self. The police raid his illicit distillery and destroy his underground business. He is now a wanted man.

Looka is desperate, without money to buy the medicines he needs to relieve his unbearable pain. He has to kill to obtain them and is then on the run. Seeking refuge, he hides in Amma's hut. The police track him down. While trying to resist, Benwa and Looka are badly beaten and arrested. During the struggle Amma has a miscarriage. Benwa's teenaged bride is left alone and helpless.

The next morning Anna arrives to find his home in ruins. The warehouse owner who has loaned them the premises wants them to leave at once because of the scandal of the police raid.

Meanwhile the authorities order the slum to be demolished. A bulldozer razes the slum to the ground.

The film is episodic in nature and despite its narrative structure does not have a conventional story form. Its canvas is large. Everyday events are reproduced to show life in a big city and the slums that line its streets. They are dirty and diseased places, where the neighbour's chicken is stolen for a celebration, an unwanted baby is dumped into a garbage bin, and a sad and skinny whore walks the streets to support an ailing father. For Amma, who wanted little, the circle of life is vicious and complete.

Uma da Cunha

Chamanya and other slum dwellers left with nothing but meagre belongings.

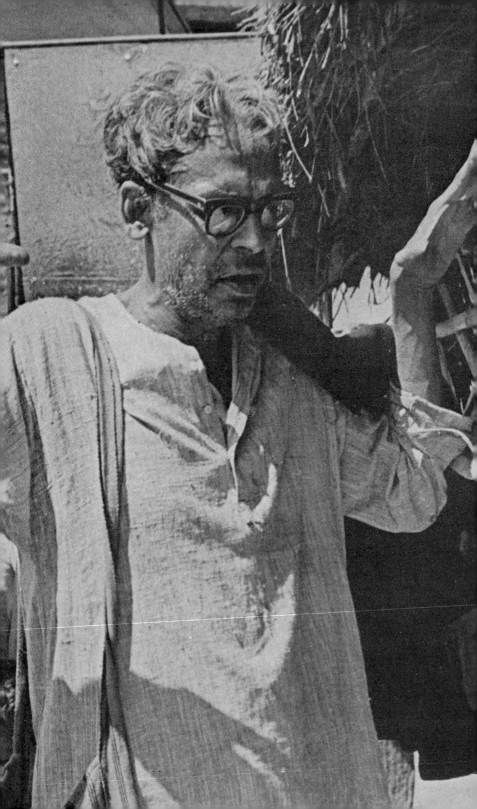

RITWIK GHATAK

Ghatak is by far the most masculine director working in the Indian Cinema today. He has an instinctive feel for the angle, the locale, the dialogue and the key in which a scene is conceived.

Gurudas Bhattacharya
Kino (Calcutta)
October 1967

When a significant work appears in any art form, something happens to the entire tradition of that art. The emergence of Ritwik Ghatak was such a phenomenon in the Indian film.

His deep loyalty to the tradition of his craft and its environment influenced his own work, which, in turn, enriched the tradition itself. This is to be expected of a man who was aware of the affinity between collective consciousness and mythology and the juxtaposition of the two as the source of all authentic human emotions and responses. At an appropriate level, all his films bear this mark of an artist trying to relate individual situations to the larger historical perspective which unleashed the original impulse for their birth. His mind is populated by memories of all that have been and are likely to be in the future. So all his major characters have individual histories of their own. Definite forebears, a place in the social strata, a perception of its mores and an awareness of the contemporary reality, however remote it may be from its distant origin. No hero or heroine is an accident or a freak, suspended in attractive ambiguity. Because Ghatak had too much reality to contend with in his life.

Born and raised in Bengal, a chronically orphan State in Eastern India where political and social turbulence tended to acquire surrealistic intensity and not infrequently, pathetic purposelessness, Ghatak roamed the fetid, forlorn villages of the land in his youth, hoping to bring the theatre to the immobile masses by staging, directing and even acting in plays wherever an audience happened to be available. Then came the Second World War. Of all things, American bombers over the timid skies of Bengal on their missions to Burma; the independence of India from British colonial rule; and finally, the partition of Bengal and the traumatic flight of refugees across a border that ran down their own backyards.

While the blight of the decade failed to brutalise the bemused Bengalis, it brought a certain ferocity to Ghatak's sensitivity which had so far been sharp but undistinguished. It was thus in the fifties that new stirrings of the urge for a more controllable form of self-expression initiated Ghatak into the film medium. And he burst upon the scene with *Ajantrik* (The Mechanical Man), a tender, pathetic story of a taxi driver of agrarian background straining to integrate himself with his unfriendly life through the medium of an industrial device, a battered car in the throes of death.

Satyajit Ray's haunting classic, *Pather Panchali* (Song of the Road), was a recent experience at that time, portraying the disintegration of rural Bengal with the hard poignance of a D. H. Lawrence. *Ajantrik,* almost at the same time, came to reinforce with a new thrust, this revaluation of Indian cinema. It was to become a seminal force in the development of the medium. The rest is un-

75

known history. Because very little of the new, committed film of India is familiar even within the country itself, let alone outside. But that is a different story.

Ghatak did not have the patience to be a neo-classicist. He was a representative citizen, close to the grass roots, earthy, with a permanent stubble of beard and the acrid smoke of leaf tobacco curling up his Dostoevskian visage, a disarming spectacle to editors eager to interview him.

Ghatak felt uncomfortable, one imagines, to repeat the formula of success. So he took risks in every film, to make it different, in characters, situations, treatment and sound track. But not without an underlying unity of perception. His perception of decadence, cruelty, alienation of people from their accepted sense of security, conflicts between strangely new and absurdly familiar forces of hostility and loyalty. And in all this he nourished a mulishly stubborn belief in the validity of tragedy and the relevance of hope.

This is perhaps why he could be crude and brutal at times. He was unafraid to unmask his middle class ethos which was nearer to the red-blooded area of working class violence and unblemished by the elegant hypocrisy to which he was heir by birth. His ferocious sensitivity plunged him into an impassioned re-examination of personal relations. Immediate causes and effects never obscured his view of the deeper forces that made society behave the way it did. His probing churned up many horrors, but none dismayed him.

In a very late film, *Subarnarekha,* the name of a river that turns murderously turbulent in the rainy season in Bengal, the brutality of a scene of slaying involving a brother and a sister, is a numbing experience, but perhaps not necessary. Ghatak insisted, in the film at least, that it was so, although the brutality was crude and overdone.

His characters act out a role that has several layers of meaning. At the deeper level, it is nearly always an extension of a mythological symbol which Ghatak's fore-fathers understood to mean simple facts of life, suffering and death, but his contemporaries found confusing. This confusion was brought about by the removal of these people into a shadow world of unreality, torn away from the mainspring. A world seared by turmoil, deprivation, erosion of values and divided against itself, an agararian society hurled into the whirlpool of deliberate industrialism.

Ghatak's characters represent a Sisyphian labour of trying to adjust to a new reality without surrendering the lingering link with the roots, roots that still speak to them in a familiar language and fill part of the void that alienation creates.

Not that Ghatak resisted social change. On the contrary. He resisted the demeaning distortions of the human soul that accompanied social change. Perhaps he also believed, because of his early association with the Communist movement, that change could be engineered without robbing people of their essential goodness. His sense of human goodness was inextricably mixed up with his obsession with the fertility cult, a focal point in his film, *Meghe Dhaka Tara* (The Hidden Star). Any violation of this cult was equivalent to prostitution, a point he made so chillingly in *Subarnarekha*.

Ghatak was a man of high passion, a diminishing human trait. This passion often tended to distort his sense of proportion. Often he failed to realise when to stop. This failure on occasion, bred aesthetic infirmities in his work. Yet, deep within himself, he nurtured an astonishingly disciplined mind. He accepted the inevitability of death, despair and waste with the calm of a biologist watching the death of his bacteria under his microscope. Yet he never ever abandoned hope. He never reduced himself to abject submission, to futility. Life, to him, was too strong to be emasculated.

Meanwhile, he became a tired man and an alcoholic. He never stooped to burden others with tales of his private griefs and agonies. He was a proud man, bordering on the arrogant. He suffered immensely. He hoped prodigiously. One of the earliest, along with Satyajit Ray, he brought a heightened awareness of social relevance to the Indian cinema.

His films sought to integrate the spectrum of a life fragmented by sudden blows of forces only dimly anticipated in the recent past. He knew that the first generation of the Indian working class was recruited straight from the paddy fields of Bengal and elsewhere and inducted into factories gleaming with strange new plants and equipment with automatic or semi-automatic controls. India was in a hurry to modernise. But the hands that were to push the buttons to activate that process were not ready, not tutored. Ghatak articulated the moral anguish of this irony.

Ritwik Ghatak died of alcohol. A lonely man, but not bitter. He was too humane for that.

Nirmal Goswami

Practically all the films of Ritwik Ghatak are about the social tensions and turmoil in Bengal in Eastern India, an area which since 1947 contained the more populous part of Pakistan, and since 1972 is known as Bangladesh. It is a measure of Ghatak's artistic calibre that he turned an essentially provincial experience into an expression of universal validity. This is probably why his brief tenure on the faculty of the Film and Television Institute of India at Pune, on the western fringe of the sub-continent, exerted a profound influence on the students, some of whom were to emerge as significant film makers including Mani Kaul and Kumar Shahani. Ghatak's music was an integral part of the language of his film, a discipline he had been initiated into by Ustad Allauddin Khan, one of the greatest exponents of classical Indian music. Unusual control over the medium of his art combined with a disarming degree of personal charm and modesty made Ritwik Ghatak a cult figure in his lifetime.

AJANTRIK
(The Mechanical Man)

Bimal's taxi splashes on a wayside madman.

1958 B&W/102 mins/Bengali
Direction/Screenplay
Ritwik Ghatak
Camera
Dinen Gupta
Music
Ustad Ali Akbar Khan
Players
*Kali Bannerji (Bimal),
Gyanesh Mukherjee
(the mechanic),
Deepak (the boy),
Gangapada Basu
(the boy's uncle),
Kajal Gupta (young woman),
Anil Chatterjee (her lover),
Keshto Mukherji
(the mad man).*
Enquiries
*Department of Information and
Cultural Affairs,
Government of West Bengal,
Writer's Building,
Calcutta.*

Bimal is a taxi driver in a small provincial town. He works a circuit that includes some mining and industrial areas in Eastern India with concentrated pockets of tribal inhabitants. The landscape reveals dry rocks, bad roads, desolate fields and occasionally, great, ancient trees. Bimal lives alone. The taxi, Jagatdal, is his only companion. It's a battered old Ford limping on decrepit limbs, uncertain brakes, erratic ignition, forgetful headlights, but to Bimal, the apple of his eye, almost the purpose of his life. Full of a precarious pride, he sits in the car at the local railroad station, waiting for a fare. Ranged alongside Jagatdal is an array of contemporary Chevrolet and Pontiac models, all in the prime of youth.

His days and nights stretch out on the road delivering passengers from one point to another. His life, a kaleidoscope of episodes brought about by brief encounters with men and women riding behind him. Once, it's a man and girl, obviously enroute to an assignation. Bimal deposits them at a motel and forgets all about them. A few days later the girl becomes his lone passenger, subdued, brooding, her worries obviously out of control. Bimal figures out the scene. The man has disappeared. The cabby brings her to the railroad station, buys her a ticket and puts her on the train. The train pulls out of view, revealing a forlorn

Bimal mourning, momentarily, the departure of a stranger. Another time, it's an elderly man in a desperate hurry to catch a train to be in time to see a dear one near death. Bimal makes it just in time. The passenger expresses his gratitude.

Once, it's a group of tribals off the train, wanting to go to their secluded village. Bimal decides to get lost in this idyllic surrounding.

Bimal knows that his car is dying. He spends hours tinkering with the old workhorse. By turns, it is his slave and his son, a son he nurtures like a heart. He orders costly spares hoping to rebuild the car's disintegrating faculties and put it back on the road. He talks to the car. Comforts it. Promises it a resurrected life. All he hears, however, is the death rattle. Finally, the silence of death. Jagatdal is very dead.

A merchant arrives to claim the corpse he will sell as junk and enables Bimal to pay back the loan he has incurred in ordering the futile spares.

The din rises in Bimal's house. Jagatdal is being dismembered. The mortal remains of Jagatdal are taken away on a bullock cart, a coffin to Bimal.

Nirmal Goswami

Filmography

1952 **NAGARIK (The Citizen)**
B&W/120 mins/Bengali
Lead players: Satendra Bhattacharya, Sova Sen
Kali Bannerjee, Ketaki Devi.

Ramu unemployed, lives with his parents, sister Gita and kid brother, Pintu. The sister's marriage and the brother's schooling are major problems. Ramu determinedly tries for a job. He falls in love with Uma, which gives his life a purpose. Sagar comes to live with the family as a paying guest and becomes a rival. Ramu and Uma drift apart. Ramu's father dies. Uma's sister becomes a prostitute. The family decide to move to a working class neighbourhood. Strains of the 'Communist Internationale' fill the sound track.

1959 **BARI THEKE PALIYE (The Runaway)**
B&W/123 mins/Bengali
Lead players: Pram Bhattarak Lahiri, Padma Devi,
Sailen Ghosh.

Kanchan, a little village boy enjoys escapades away from home in a big city and finds many an accidental benefactor... Haridas, a teacher turned street peddler, an aging maidservant, a gangster masquerading as a magician, a cart pusher, and Mini, a small girl with wealthy parents. Kanchan is restored to his parents in the village. He tells his father that the city is an aberration; there's nothing like home.

1960 **MEGHE DHAKA TARA (The Hidden Star)**
B&W/120 mins/Bengali
Lead players: Supriya Chowdhury, Anil Chatterjee,
Gita Ghatak.
Nita, the protagonist, dies a slow death, orchestrated by a
remorseless chain of misfortunes. In a family driven by abject
poverty, Nita is the only earning member. Because of it she
sacrifices the one man in her life to her younger sister,
Gita. An unemployed brother, devoted to music, becomes a
famous singer. Another brother finds a job. Just when
fortune smiles, Nita is struck by tuberculoses and removed
to a sanatorium in the mountains. The brother sings
about the joys of life to a sister in the throes of death.

KOMAL GANDHAR (E Flat)
B&W/110 mins/Bengali
Lead players: Supriya Chowdhury, Avinash Bannerjee,
Anil Chatterjee, Bijon Bhattacharya.
Bhrigu's mission in life is to reach the people through
theatre. Amusua, a girl interested in his work, tries to help
him. A particular play is affected because of Shanta, a
member of the group, who has differing ideas about their
cause. She finally defects. Bhrigu is ridiculed for the
failure of the play. Amusua stands by him. They face the
future with courage and hope.

1962 **SUBARNAREKHA**
B&W/132 mins/Bengali
Lead players: Madhabi Mukherjee, Satindra Bhattacharya,
Abhi Bhattacharya, Jahar Roy
Ishwar works in a foundry on the bank of the river
Subarnarekha in Eastern India. He lives with his sister Sita
and with Abhiram, an orphan, who grow up and fall in love
with each other. They run away to Calcutta and live in
dire poverty made worse by the birth of a son, Binu. One
day Abhiram is lynched to death and Sita is forced into
prostitution. Ishwar, a lonely and weary man, is in town

Still from
Titash Ekti
Nadir Naam
(A River Named Titash).

seeking pleasure. The brother meets his sister as a customer. The humiliation drives Sita to suicide. Ishwar returns to the river bank with his little nephew Binu.

1973 TITASH EKTI NADIR NAAM (A River Named Titash)
(Made in Bangladesh) Approximately 140 mins.
Lead players: Rosy, Sufia, Kabari Chowdhury,
Ravi Sarkar
Titash, a river in Bangladesh, is drying up. Its fishing community is disintegrating. The river is threatened by encroaching sands. The fisherfolk seek work elsewhere. People from the city come to claim the land to turn it into a paddy field. Basanti, a lonely woman, is the last remaining member of the fishing community still clutching at a way of life which is doomed.

1974 JUKTI, TAKKO AAR GAPPO
(Reason, Debate and a Tale)
B&W/120 mins/Bengali
Lead players: Ritwik Ghatak, Tripti Mitra, Saonli Mitra,
Bijon Bhattacharya
Episodes in the life of Neelkantha, the protagonist, reveal the moral alienation of Bengali intellectuals of the early seventies, the social impact of the war of liberation in Bangladesh and the agrarian tensions created by the Naxalite movement—a militant communist group—in Eastern India. Neelakantha, about to be reunited with an estranged wife, is accidentally shot by a police bullet. There are other deaths among men and women who are in love.

SOME IMPORTANT DOCUMENTARIES
1955 Oroan (a tribal group)
1963 Ustad Allauddin Khan (a noted musician)
1964-65 Fear (short film)
1967 Scientists of Tomorrow
1970 Chhao Dance of Purulia
1970 Amaar Lenin (A short film which has been publicly screened in the USSR but not in India)
1970 Yeh Kyon (short film) Hindi
1971 Where the Padma Flows (partly in colour)
1975 Ram Kinkar (Ghatak died before completing the film)

SCREENPLAYS
1955 Musafir (The Traveller) Hindi
1955 Madhumati Hindi
1960 Swarlipi (Musical Notation)
1962 Kunwari Mon
1963 Dwiper Naam Tiyarang (An Island Named Tiyarang)
1965 Rajkanya (The Princess)

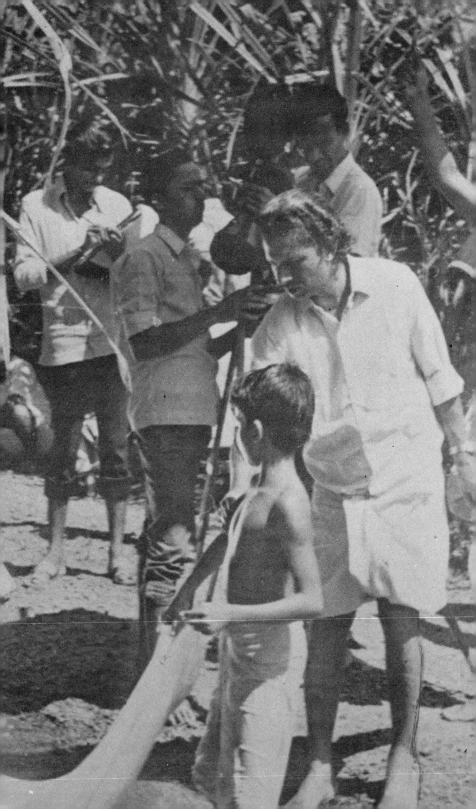

ADOOR GOPALAKRISHNAN

It is one of those ironies of life that a man totally disinterested in films should one day be noted for it. Adoor Gopalakrishnan's sole interest from the age of eight was centred on the stage. He wanted to write, direct and act in plays. The theatrical fervour is understandable in a person with his family and cultural background.

Adoor is the name of a small town in Kerala, one which is known for its performing arts, including *Kathakali,* the magnificent, vivid and stylised dance drama that is indigenous to it. Adoor, the film maker, hails from this village. (Prefixing the name of the village before one's name is an old practice among *Kathakali* artists). Adoor's family for generations were patrons and practitioners of *Kathakali.* In this art form, details of individual dancers gradually emerge in lamplight out of total darkness. Adoor sees in it the embryo of pure cinema, a scope for varied use of close-ups and editing.

After graduating in 1961 with Political Science from Gandhigram Rural Institute, Madurai, Adoor had a short spell of government duty. He talks with characteristic reserve of his idealistic Gandhian phase when he took to wearing *khadi* (coarse home-spun cloth). The simplicity persists in his life style and in the humanism of his work.

Chance led him to film. Unable to join Delhi's National School of Drama because of his ignorance of Hindi, he opted for the scriptwriting and direction course at the Film Institute in Pune. His years at the Institute and exposure to the grammar and aesthetics of films changed his perspective.

Adoor eschews esoteric technique though film is a personal medium for him. He declares, "I like an audience and I want to be understood by it," but is not prepared to make "any concessions to popular audience tastes."

Fully aware that he and those like him with a strong uncompromising style were unwelcome in the commercial arena, he took the lead in forming the first film cooperative in India. 'Chitralekha' was a unique and challenging concept aimed at financing and distributing good quality features and documentaries. Today it is a sprawling, impressive place with an infrastructure that provides equipment, studio and screening facilities for film makers.

Recalling the early days, Adoor says, "Living in a tiny lodge room, we were struggling to start the Cooperative. I had a typewriter and a scooter. I was the typist, office clerk, peon and officer. That's how 'Chitralekha' began . . ."

Adoor had scripted, directed (and photographed a few) twenty-four documentary films. The best known among these are *Guru Chengannur* (on the great *Kathakali* artist), *Yakshagana* (on the folk theatre of Karnataka) and *Chola Heritage* (on South India's temple architecture and sculpture).

Adoor made his first feature film with a loan from the Film Finance Corporation. *Swayamvaram,* (One's Own Choice) shows the contrast between idealism and reality providing an unthinkable dimension to a tale of runaway lovers facing harsh economic truths after the euphoria of first love.

Adoor describes the film as "a trip from illusion to reality." Its story of the despair of young rebels is told sensitively without an overlay of sentimentality or pathos. The reality of small-town life, the struggle for livelihood, the unvarnished vignettes of prostitutes and lecherous smugglers develop naturally, encompassing and commenting on the individual fate of the couple. The girl, Sita, with her lover dead and a baby to raise, stares at the bolted door as a thunderstom rages outside. Adoor leaves Sita there, to face an uncertain future. The film won the President's Gold Medal for Best Film, Best Director, Best Cameraman and Best Actress.

Swayamvaram was a startling film for its time. It tackled a taboo subject and sympathised with unconventional, untraditional behaviour and a woman's dilemma in particular. It was an instant success and propelled Adoor to national and international recognition.

Adoor reveals a mixture of modesty and egoism when he says he did not want to marry after having made a name for himself. Appropriately, he made his own choice when he married Sunanda while he was shooting *Swayamvaram.* They now have a seven-year-old daughter who loves films and is an admirer of her father.

Adoor is quiet, sensitive by nature, yet fiercely adamant in his stance. This, perhaps, leads to misconceptions and controversy. He confides rarely, if at all. He tends to keep his worries, disappointments and feeling to himself, at times to his own disadvantage.

Adoor suddenly quit 'Chitralekha' in 1980 maintaining a strict, stern silence for his reasons. He won't talk of what must have been a painful experience. Thereafter he could not find a financier nor would he go looking for one.

Adoor took five years to start his second feature film, *Kodiyettam* (Ascent). He says, "I allow my film a kind of organic development. My films keep evolving till I take out the final print." The universality of the theme, of a man coming to terms with himself, and the sincerity of the director, were unusual traits in films of that time. Kerala was churning out titillating films masquerading as realism; and its "sex wave" (the press labelled it so) was invading even the non-traditional markets. The wide appeal of *Kodiyettam* with its simple, modest approach and home-spun theme was, to say the least, unexpected.

Kodiyettam also testifies to the pervading influence of the matrilineal Nair culture to which Adoor is heir. Adoor carefully recreates the Nair ethos, culled from memories of his village. He says of *Kodiyettam,* "Though I live in this city I cannot be free from the temples, festivals, ceremonies, rituals practised in my village and the people who lived around it. It is my story, it is my experience. Each and every frame is from my heart."

Adoor lives in a house which adheres to the sprawling quadrangular structure (the *Nalukettu*) around an inner courtyard. This transplantation of the typical Nair family mansion to the city suburbs of Trivandrum, where petro-dollars have sprouted alien concrete structures, is revealing of the duality in the man.

In Adoor's house, sitting under the shade of a mango tree or on the extension resembling the temple *Anakottil* (where elephants are stabled), we feel we are in a temple of South Kerala. It is here that he thinks creatively of his films. Lying on the floor, he reflects on the past, resurrecting those dead people who bequeathed a way of life peculiar to their times.

Adoor is a finicky perfectionist. He sits through many nights at the editing table worrying over that one extra frame. He is choosy to a fine point, turning his material over and over till it is just right. That's why he takes time over his films.

Adoor has made only two feature films in fifteen years. The gap is inconsequential compared to their impact. *Swayamvaram* gave Kerala its initial impetus to explore its own rich, deep-rooted culture. *Kodiyettam* revived that need when it was required. These two films are in constant demand in India and internationally. They put Kerala on the world map. What Ray is to India, Adoor in his way is to Kerala.

With his confidence and strength of purpose, Adoor is now at work on his third film, *Elippathayam* (The Mouse Trap). This year he was appointed director on the Board of the National Film Development Corporation, India's apex film body.

V. Sasikumar

Adoor Gopalakrishnan frowns in concentration and attempts to understand a language and style outside his native Kerala. Suddenly the crisscross lines clear and he smiles with the clarity of a child. But, cross swords with him and if he is a friend, he relapses into a near sullen silence . . . for an extended period of time. Or, if you are a close friend, he will attack headlong in a flurry of gestures and words. And then smile . . . a confident smile that makes it clear to you that he is right, you are wrong.

KODIYETTAM
(Ascent)

The new bride angrily scolds children who want her husband to play with them.

1977/B&W/118 mins/Malayalam
Direction/Script/Story/Dialogue
Adoor Gopalakrishnan
Camera
Ravi Verma
Produced by
Kulathoor Bhaskaran Nair
Art Direction
Sivan
Editing
M. Moni
Players
Gopi (Sankarankutty),
Lalitha (Sathamma), Kaviyoor
Ponamma (Kamalamma)
Enquiries
Chitralekha Film Cooperative.
Trivandrum 695017, Kerala.

The film presents a vivid account of a country bumpkin coming to terms with his marriage. It touches on village life, its rituals, its occupations, its people, its family relationships. The last provides the main interest and theme of the film.

The film is about a young man called Sankarankutty who is taken up with aimless pursuits and childish pleasures. He eats gluttonously, plays with children, idles at the tea-shop, joins wastrels for a drink. He revels in the spectacle, the crowds and the opportunity of quick earning offered by temple festivals. He lives by the money his sister (a servant) sends him, and by helping in household chores round the village. There is a lonely childless widow who takes a maternal interest in him. Sankarankutty is aghast to find she is having an affair with a married man.

For all his aimless ways, people in the village quite like Sankarankutty. He is invariably made the scapegoat. He is the one to be caught with a gambling wheel during a raid. A friend intervenes and the police release him. Sankarankutty is easy in any situation. Detention within the prison gave him a good view of the temple fireworks. The indignity of being arrested does not worry him.

Finally, Sankarankutty is prevailed upon to marry. The custom is that a marriage broker takes the prospective bridegroom to the girl's family and they are all fed a sumptuous meal cooked by the girl as a test of her usefulness in marriage. Sankarankutty overeats to the point of falling into a stupor and vaguely conveys his consent when others insist.

Once married, his lessons in growing up begin. His wife, disgusted by his neglect even when she is about to have a baby, returns to her parents. His sister can no longer provide for him because she lives with a lover. The widow who was kind to him commits suicide because of her seedy love affair.

Sankarankutty finds himself alone and miserable. He gets drunk. Then he takes his first steady job as an assistant to a truck-driver. He observes life seriously for once, and sees what marriage can mean and what deception it can contain.

The truck-driver is hardworking and responsible, in his own way. He is a strict disciplinarian but breaks rules all the same. He drinks heavily, off duty. He is a stern father and a cold husband. He keeps a mistress on the side whose fidelity he suspects. Even in this triangle, Sankarankutty senses the tensions growing out of mutual distrust. He begins to evaluate himself. He realises that he has treated his wife unfairly. He woos her back, and is at last able to communicate with her.

The film has no background music. It uses the natural sounds of Kerala's countryside, ranging from the majestic drums of *Kathakali* to the strident mooing of cows.

Adoor Gopalakrishnan is scrupulous about the authenticity of his material. He has an exact eye for faces and has drawn exemplary performances from his actors. Gopi, in particular, is remarkably astute as Sankarankutty. He fidgets, he grins, and wears a look of doleful befuddlement which makes him vulnerable and appealing.

People are observed with a fine sense of humour. It is amusing to see the bovine haste with which Sankarankutty reaches for a second helping . . . his angry growl at children using his pate for a game . . . his childish curiosity about all that is obvious.

"I know that the repeated shots of people eating may be off-putting," says Adoor, "but I cannot do without them. They are a fixed daily ritual that is part of our way of life." The film does convey the fact that the only communication between husband and wife can be the serving of food. The rest is then silence or suffering, unless the wife becomes less a servant and more a person.

The film is full of fine observation that transcends its Indian setting to make a statement on that evergreen theme of a man finding identity and possibly maturity. Pic is slow but always revealing and full of poetic insights into the characters, place and time giving it universal impact.

Gene Moskowitz
Variety (U.S.A.)
January 31, 1979

Uma da Cunha

Filmography

1972 **SWAYAMVARAM (One's Own Choice)**
B&W/130 mins/Malayalam
Lead Players: Sharda, Madhu, Thikkurissi, Adoor Bhavani
A remarkably courageous first film which deals with the story of Viswam and Sita, a young couple intensely in love. They live together in a small town without being married. The focus is on the vulnerable predicament of the woman. Viswam gets a job as a temporary lecturer in a tutorial college sacrificing his literary ambitions. Their ecstacy and minor estrangements have to survive harsh economic realities when Viswam loses his job. A prostitute, a helpful older woman and the dishonest prosperous smuggler, covertly interested in Sita—these are the elements of the seedy environment. Without an overlay of romanticism, the director shows his protagonists experiencing despondency and alienation. Viswam dies leaving Sita with a baby. The callousness of contemporary society forcing them to a death-in-life forms the thematic core.

Adoor Gopalakrishnan at work on his new film.

1977　**KODIYETTAM (Ascent)**

1980　**THE CHOLA HERITAGE** (documentary)
Col/16 mins/English
The film traces the development of temple architecture, sculpture, bronze casting and painting of the Chola period (eighth and ninth century).

Currently working on:
ELIPPATHAYAM (Mouse Trap).
Lead players: Sharda, Karamana, Jalaja, Rajam K. Nair.
Unni, the pivotal character, inherits a burden of ancestral self-indulgence which only a bygone exploitative social order could afford. He is unable to cope with changes taking place around him. He withdraws into a state of apathy.

GIRISH KARNAD

Girish Karnad wants to
form a cadre of trained film
makers capable of working
in the industry ... he would
very much want to mix very
closely the disciplines —
cinema and television, also
obliging the students to
study simultaneously
editing, direction and
acting. They could then
specialise later. Girish
Karnad would also like
to see the students go out
and discover the world
beyond the gates of the
School and join
contemporary India.

Louis Marcorelles
Le Monde (France)
January 1976 (written when
Karnad was Director of the
Film Institute at Pune).

To start with, a statement of fact: Girish Karnad is the
only major Indian film maker to have a matching status
in the theatre. There are other playwright-film makers
as well as directors in both media. But Karnad's work,
taken as a whole, shows a complexity of artistic purpose
that is rarely found in the work of any of the others.

Soon after Karnad made his film *Ondanondu Kaladalli*
(Once Upon a Time), he completed his fifth play *'Hittina
Hunja'* (Cock of Dough), based on an old Jain legend. In
fact, he has often said that he is primarily a playwright,
and only then a film maker.

Such statements have often tended to baffle critics.
Especially those unable to put together his work in a
single critical perspective or to see it as a manifestation of
deeper undercurrents of change and development within him.

These undercurrents of change can be seen in all his
work since he first achieved national prominence with his
second play *'Tughlaq'* (1964), which immediately set him on
the top rung of playwrights and helped revive a dying
Indian theatre in the sixties. The play, based on the life
of the despot-visionary Sultan Mohammed Tughlaq, made
subtle allusions to the then Prime Minister of India,
Jawaharlal Nehru. Says Karnad, "We belonged to the first
generation of independent India. The crumbling of the
Nehruvian dream in the last days of the Nehru era, the
disillusionment of people everywhere with his inability to
grapple with the reality after the promises, and the waning
charisma of the man — all this struck me as having more
than a passing resemblance to the time of Tughlaq. After
I wrote it I found that playwrights all over the country —
Badal Sarkar, Mohan Rakesh, Tendulkar — had the same
preoccupations as mine. Suddenly we were a 'movement'."

Following the success of *'Tughlaq'* Karnad was settling
down to what to all intents appeared a sedentary executive-
litterateur's life (working with the Oxford University Press
in Madras). But it was clearly not for him and he suddenly
left the job and went to his native Dharwar to re-acquaint
himself with his roots. "I was at a sort of crossroads in
my life," recalls Karnad, "I even planned to go to a village
and work there." But one day he came across the manuscript of an unpublished novel, *'Samskara'* (Funeral Rites)
by U. R. Ananthamurthy. "I was so struck by the visual
power of the book that I felt it had to be turned into a
film. Until then films had not interested me at all, but
after reading *'Samskara'* I started studying the medium.
I talked about it to everyone I met. I knew Pattabhi Rama
Reddy to whom I read the book out in English." Pattabhi
agreed to make the film and thus, Karnad found himself
scripting and then acting in *Samskara*. The film, which
everyone had warned would prove a disaster, was first
banned by the Censors and then went on to win the
President's Gold Medal as the Best Indian Film of 1970.

Soon after *Samskara,* he received another offer — to make *Vamsha Vriksha* (The Family Tree) with a fellow theatre personality, B. V. Karanth. *Kaadu* (The Forest) followed and suddenly the playwright found himself at the vanguard of the now famed Kannada "New Wave," and praised as one of the most promising film makers in the country.

By the time B.V.Karanth's *Chomana Dudi* (Choma's Drum) followed Karnad's *Kaadu,* the Kannada "New Wave" had effectively wrested for itself the reputation for being the centre of serious cinema in India. But soon after, the movement seemed to start losing its sense of direction. Karnad took a long holiday from making films and accepted a totally different assignment — a Government of India offer to be Director of the Film and Television Institute of India.

"At the FTII," says Karnad, "I was more like a student than a Director. I got my first chance to study film making systematically, to see film classics and meet film theoreticians." Two years later, he moved to Bombay. He worked with Shyam Benegal. He acted in Benegal's *Nishant* (Night's End) and *Manthan* (The Churning); wrote scripts for his *Bhumika* (The Role) and *Kondura* (The Boon). Later he acted a memorable role in Basu Chatterji's *Swami* (The Saint). The FTII and Bombay experience must have been formative, because when he made his next film, *Ondanondu Kaladalli* (Once Upon a Time), it proved his most finely crafted film yet. Karnad has often described it as his tribute to the great master, Akira Kurosawa.

By this time, Karnad's work showed a maturity which indicated that he had intellectually come to terms with himself.

Karnad has had to withstand the reactionary blast that every major artist who decides to look at Indian society objectively has to face from conservative circles in India. His first two films were attacked as "anti-brahmin," though Karnad himself is brahmin by birth. *Kaadu,* however, has nothing to do with caste. It is essentially an exploration of violence in feudal Indian society, an analysis of its socio-economic causes. *Ondanondu Kaladalli,* on the other hand, is an action film, where the socio-economic elements are hidden carefully under the almost simplistic structure of a swash-buckler. A Rhodes Scholar from Oxford, the unorthodoxy and wide range of influences he brings to bear on his work have often tended to puzzle or irritate his son-of-the-soil colleagues.

In fact, in his youth, Karnad was bothered by his cosmopolitan background that seemed to make him rootless. "It used to worry me that I couldn't choose my subjects from an authentic Kannada context, because I wasn't from a Karnataka village. In fact, my upbringing has been closer to Marathi culture than to Kannada. This doesn't bother me any more though. After all, rooted or rootless, it's a question of making the best of what one is."

This background may explain why his original plays and film scripts have mainly been concerned with myths and history. The film scripts which have dealt with modern India have all been based on novels by other writers. He reacts to myth, legend or history with more intensity than to contemporary problems.

Even in his films, he has tended to move away from the neo-realistic form with its mirror realism, which has become the norm in New Indian Cinema. This has enabled him to bring to his films a mythic sensibility, a vast storehouse of unexplored possibilities. Take for instance the fantasy-like ending of *Kaadu:* the little child Kitti is lost in the forest; at night he hears the search party calling out to him. Kitti does not respond because he is sure the calls are being made by *Alu Koogina Hakki* (Bird-with-Human-Voice). The bird is reputed to destroy those who respond to its calls. The boy prefers to remain lost. The previous scene had shown the police entering the village, headlights and all. It is a daring transition, but Karnad carries it off.

With the definition of realism often degenerating into pallid imitations of Satyajit Ray or overt gestures of Communist symbolism, it is only Karnad who has succeeded in using the rich mythic lore to so devastating an effect. It is ultimately this confidence, the high technical competence (he is arguably the finest script-writer in the country today) have made it possible for him to do what could be a phenomenal achievement for an artist, certainly in the present context of Indian cinema — to establish for himself his own tradition.

Ashish Rajadhyaksha

Girish Karnad's career so far has been characterised by restlessness; a refusal to settle down in one job or place — which is in marked contrast to the calm, composed image he projects. In fact, Girish himself has often said that his main fear has always been of being trapped in a given image of himself. A graduate in Mathematics and Statistics, he went to Oxford as a Rhodes Scholar to study Philosophy, Politics and Economics. Karnad was president of the Oxford Union. At Oxford, he decided he would never make a poet and wrote his first play — in the Kannada language. Then unexpectedly, he went into film acting.

"I have been very fortunate in the opportunities I got. When I returned to India I had decided not to take a nine-to-five job. For an average Indian of my age, I was in a lucky position. In the arts, India is a land of truly phenomenal opportunities. But most people with talent are unable to use them because of their financial or family burdens. My parents were well-off or could feed me if necessary. They certainly did not expect me to look after them. I have no younger brothers to educate or settle, no sisters who have to be married off. I decided it would be stupid not to use this freedom. It meant only one major sacrifice. I could not afford to get married. So I didn't."

As unexpectedly, he got married in 1980. His wife, Saraswathy Ganapathy, is a neo-natologist in the New York University Medical Centre. They had known each other for fourteen years.

KAADU
(The Forest)

1973/Col/123 mins/Kannada
Direction/Screenplay
Girish Karnad
Produced by
K. N. Narayan
Story
Srikrishna Alanahalli
Camera
Govind Nihalani
Editing
P. Bhaktavasalam
Art Direction/Music
B. V. Karanth
Players
G. S. Nataraj (Kitti),
Amrish Puri (Chandre Gowda),
Nandini (Kamli), Lokesh
(Shivganga), Kalpana Sirur
(Kalyani).
Enquiries
L. N. Combines,
Malani,
4 Lakshmi Road,
Shanti Nagar,
Bangalore 560 027.
Tel: 53756

The boy Kitti in the courtyard of his new village home.

Kitti, a ten-year-old boy, comes from the city to stay with a childless aunt named Kamli, and his uncle, Chandre Gowda, in a remote village called Koppal in Karnataka. He adores his aunt. Their relationship resembles that of mother and son. Kitti is also fascinated by the awesome forest between his village and the neighbouring one named Hosur.

Kitti becomes aware of the hostility that exists between the two villages, despite their interdependence. Kitti attends school every day in Hosur. He notices that his uncle goes every night to Hosur to visit his mistress, the widow Basakka. Kitti senses the pain this act of desertion causes his forlorn aunt.

Kamli persuades a frightened Kitti to accompany her late one night to consult a witch-doctor. She takes part in a ritual sacrifice meant to win back her husband's love.

Kitti's playmate is his cousin Nagi. One day he spies a couple making love in the clearing. He recognises the man as a Koppal villager, Kencha, but not the woman. Later he recovers an ear-ring from the same place.

At night the Koppal elders hold a meeting called *Nyaya* to jointly censure Kencha for having seduced a Hosur wife, of which Kitti has first-hand evidence, but keeps silent.

Kencha lives in Koppal but works for a Hosur landlord

called Shivganga. Shivganga noisily disrupts the meeting, ostensibly to protect his servant. In fact he begrudges Chandre Gowda the land he wanted for himself. His insulting the Koppal *Nyaya* and deriding Chandre Gowda for his affair with a Hosur woman leads to a violent clash. Gowda lashes him publicly with a whip.

Exhaustion and the delay prevent Gowda from visiting Basakka that night. Kamli ascribes the change to witchcraft, and is thankful.

The *Nyaya* infringement by a Hosur man and his subsequent public humiliation leads to covert recrimination. Kitti's pet dog is found poisoned. The servants' share of crop, stored to last the year in Gowda's backyard, is set on fire. The Koppal elders do not investigate or retaliate, afraid to further endanger their crumbling social norms. Calling the police will demean and destroy their autonomy and status.

Kitti comes to know that the woman he spied on was his cousin, Nagi's step-mother, Kalyani. He contrives to return the incriminating ear-ring he had found. Kalyani and her lover Kencha escape from their respective villages via the city bus. The bus is seen by the villages as an access to the outside world and its corrupting influences.

Hosur residents, wanting to curb erupting violence, attempt a reconciliation through their annual water sport *Okali,* to which they invite their Koppal neighbours. But the seething Koppal servants provoke a fight which develops into a relentless riot.

The wounded Gowda is bedridden. He receives a frantic warning from his mistress to stay home that night as the Hosur villagers are out to kill him. He rebelliously answers that he will visit her the following night.

Panic-stricken, Kamli attempts a second nocturnal visit to the witch-doctor, this time more to save her husband's life. She is waylaid and assaulted by Shivganga and his men, while Kitti hides and watches in horror. Kamli dies as a result.

Koppal villagers, roused to fury, raid Hosur that night in a full-scale attack. In the blood bath that follows, Shivganga is killed. As a futile gesture of honour, Gowda places a mark of blood on his dead wife's forehead.

The dreaded police arrive and arrest Gowda and other younger men who caused the rampage. A police outpost is set up, with a fine imposed on the two villages in order to maintian it. The villagers lose their right to conduct *Nyaya*.

Kitti's parents arrive to take him back. He hides in the forest, petrified because of its legend of *Alu Koogina Hakki*—a menacing bird which calls out your name; and if you answer it, you will vomit blood till you die. He ignores the search party calling out to him...

The film is seen through the eyes of the child, Kitti. It concerns three themes: the tragic destruction of village life and values; the martyrdom of Kamli, victim of rivalry and revenge; and finally, the mind of a sensitive boy who finds the forest symbolic of an adult world.

Perhaps the most striking feature of the film, though, is the way it achieves novelistic density without sacrificing cinema in the least ... Effortlessly and almost imperceptibly, it conveys a fascinating wealth of detail.

Tom Milne
**Monthly Film Bulletin
(U.K.) June 1977**

ONDANONDU KALADALLI
(Once Upon A Time)

1978/Col/156 mins/Kannada
Direction
Girish Karnad
Produced by
G. N. Lakshmipathy,
K. N. Narayan
Script
Krishna Basrur,
Girish Karnad
Music
Bhaskar Chandavarkar
Lyrics
Chandrasekhar Kambar
Dialogue
G. B. Joshi
Art Direction
Jayoo, Nachiket
Camera
A. K. Bir
Editing
P. Bhaktavatsalam
Players
Shankar Nag (Gandugali),
Sunder Krishna Urs
(Permadi), Akshata Rao
(Savantri), Sushilendra
Joshi (Jayakeshi), Ajit
Saldanha (Permadi's son,
Iraga), Rekha Sabnis
(Permadi's wife), Anil Thakkar
(Kapardi), Vasant Rao
Nakod (Maranayaka).
Enquiries
L. N. Combines,
Malani,
4 Lakshmi Road,
Shanti Nagar,
Bangalore 560 027.
Tel: 53756

The newly-inducted mercenary, Gandugali, terrorizes a villager.

The setting: medieval Karnataka, thirteenth century, after the Hoysalas and before the Vijayanagar Empire, at a time when there was no central empire holding it together. It was a balkanized State, ruled by little, greedy men, all squabbling with each other for more land and power.

In this lawless society, the skill most in demand was that of the soldier. The person most in evidence was the mercenary warrior willing to hire himself out to the highest bidder.

At once a frank tribute to Kurosawa and to the Kung-fu tradition, this is the first Indian martial arts picture. It is set in the fourteenth century (India claims to be the birthplace of martial arts created by the Buddhist priests who were not allowed to carry arms but had to protect themselves against marauding bandits on the roads). In a supremely enjoyable film, Karnad brings to the genre historical authenticity, human characters, a strong narrative sense and some brilliantly choreographed fights.

David Robinson
London Times
April 3, 1979

Not surprisingly, Karnataka of the period was known as the home of martial arts. Fortune-seeking soldiers poured into Karnataka from all over India. Kannada warriors were in demand as far away as Nepal. In Karnataka itself, the fate of the body politic was decided not by the ruler but by men, ruthless and avaricious, but matchless in battle.

The scene of action is a little *palaya* (kingdom) lying on the border between the Malnad jungles and the plains of the Deccan. Two brothers, Maranayaka and Kapardi, are the neighbouring rulers, and a ceaseless tussle is going on between them for each other's lands. Kapardi has an aging general called Permadi, whose skill and intelligence give him an edge over his brother Maranayaka.

Into this scene, already taut with mutual hatred and suspicion, walks Gandugali, a wandering mercenary. He is hired by Maranayaka. Soon Permadi realizes that he has met his match in this new, younger, more cunning and unscrupulous rival.

The encounter between Permadi and Gandugali starts like a game of chess, each trying to outguess and outsmart the other. But they also represent two distinct attitudes to life. Permadi is an "old-world" General, with a deep sense of honour and loyalty to his master. He is totally contemptuous of "hired dogs" like Gandugali, who fight for a price. On the other hand, for Gandugali, Permadi is a slightly comic figure who will not see that a warrior is condemned to lead a dog's life, risking his life for a few crumbs of bread and a nod of appreciation from his master.

"The game of chess" cannot remain casual for long. In an atmosphere where loyalty is a precious commodity and betrayal a reality hovering round the corner, Permadi and Gandugali both find themselves humiliated by their masters. A contributing factor is the jealousy of the General supplanted by Gandugali.

The two fighters form an alliance against their own masters, thus driving the two brothers into each other's

The rival General, Permadi (centre) anticipates a counter plot.

arms. Now it is an encounter between the two classes: the masters and the paid servants. Even in this life-and-death struggle, the brothers do not trust each other, and the fighters do not know when their own colleagues will stab them in the back.

Interwoven in this story of bravery and betrayal, cruelty and cowardice is the story of Jayakeshi, a young boy of about eighteen who finally ascends the throne that is rightfully his; Jayakeshi's engaging girlfriend; Permadi's brave and youthful son Iraga who dies in a futile attempt to save his family's honour; the womenfolk from the big household; and the cruel and cowardly warriors. Every once and again we glimpse, in all the violence and waste, intimate and tender moments and growing affections between individuals. At the end of the film, Jayakeshi comes to the throne, with the hope and idealism of a new generation. The fights choreographed with finesse build from the initial sword-flashing to a dazzling *Urmi* (long, flexible swords) sequence, the likes of which have not been seen in India before.

There is throughout the film the detached atmosphere of a ballad in the midst of all the ritual slaughter. The theme song, "Once Upon A Time," outlines the elemental but simple conflict of once long ago.

Filmography

1971 **VAMSHA VRIKSHA (The Family Tree)**
B&W/100 mins/Kannada
Jointly directed by Karnad and B. V. Karanth
Based on a popular novel that has a pious and humane scholar, fiercely proud of his lineage, as the central character. His young widowed daughter-in-law, after the tragic drowning of her husband, an only child, pursues her studies. Her baby son is looked after by the doting old couple. She falls in love with her English lecturer, an extrovert theatre activist. She marries him but has to give up her son to the grand-parents.

An unresolved guilt ruins her health and she is unable to bear any more children. Her grown son, now her student, refuses to acknowledge the relationship. As she is on her death bed, her old father-in-law visits her. He has renounced his wealth and heritage after accidentally discoverings his own illegitimacy.

1972 **BENDRE** (documentary)
B&W/18 mins
D. R. Bendre, now in his eighties, is considered the greatest Kannada poet of this century. The film is an attempt to see Bendre's life in terms of his poems. He lives in Dharwar, which is Karnad's home-town.

1977 **GODHULI (The Hour of the Gods)**
Col/145 mins/Hindi/Kannada versions

Lead players: Naseeruddin Shah, Kulbhushan Kharbanda, Paula Lindsay, Lakshmi Krishnamurthy

The same duo made this film in two languages, based on the novel of the same prolific novelist. It is a dramatic confrontation between East and West — the mute mother, representing the unchanging tradition of the village, and the American daughter-in-law, armed with modern technology to revolutionise dairy farming. The cow, venerated by Hindus as holy, becomes the symbol of the struggle between two ways of life.

The man is torn betwen his heritage and his belief. The American girl is defeated by the alien culture, despite her genuine and painstaking efort to understand it.

The man's plight, signified by his inability to recognize his own herd of cows, suggests that it is too late for him to get back to his roots.

1981 **(Under production) As yet untitled.**
Col/Hindi
Lead players: Shashi Kapoor, Rekha, Padmini Kolhapure, Raj Babbar, Shammi Kapoor.
An erotic comedy based on the fourth century Sanskrit classic *'Mrichhakatika'* (The Little Clay Cart). It involves a beautiful courtesan, a young girl, her husband, a villainous usurper, a nobleman, a thief . . . all getting in each other's way in plots and counterplots.

The film is scripted and directed by Karnad. Shashi Kapoor is the producer.

PLAYS IN KANNADA
1961 *Yayati* (The epic hero granted the boon of eternal youth), **1964** *Tughlaq* (The pre-Moghul King), **1970-71** *Hayavadana* (The Horse Face), **1977** *Anjumallige* (The Shy Jasmine), **1981** *Hittina Hunja* (The Cock of Dough).

SCRIPT
1971 *Samskara* (Funeral Rites), **1976** *Bhumika* (The Role) with Dubey, **1981** *Kondura* (The Boon) with Benegal and Arudra, **1981** *Kalyug* (The Machine Age) with Benegal and Dubey.

ACTED IN
1970 *Samskara* (Funeral Rites), **1971** *Vamsha Vriksha* (The Family Tree), **1975** *Nishant* (Night's End), **1976** *Manthan* (The Churning), **1976** *Kanakambara* (The Blossom), **1976** *Swami* (The Saint), **1980** *Ratnadeep* (The Jewelled Flame), **1980** *Jeevan Jyoth* (The Flame of Life), **1980** *Man Pasand* (To One's Liking), **1980** *Aasha* (Hope), **1981** *Apne Paraye* (Our Relations).

UNDER PRODUCTION
Asank (The Trusting), *Teri Arjoo* (Your Desire), *Panch Quaidi* (The Five Convicts), *Bayan Haath ka Khel),* (Child's Play), *Ahistha Ahistha* (Gradually), *Ashwamedher Ghora* (The Sacrificial Horse), *Terai* (The Foothills), *Matlabi* (The Selfish), *Mazloom* (The Downtrodden).

GIRISH KASARAVALLI

Dark, stocky, wide-sweeping forehead, large enquiring eyes, modest and unassuming, Kasaravalli keeps a low profile and seems reticent. But he is quick to take up issues and debate fiercely, if the subject is cinema, theatre or literature. The streak of stubborn independence made him break the rules of Pune's Film Institute and take time off to assist B. V. Karanth in his first film, *Choma's Drum*. Like some other serious film makers in India, Kasaravalli makes woman his protagonist ... whether it is the tragedy of Yamuna of the 1920s in *Ghatashraddha* (The Ritual), or the enigmatic and uninhibited heroine of *Akramana* (The Siege) or the violent protest of Nirmala, a teenager of today in his latest film *Mooru Darigalu* (The Three Paths).

On the western half of the South Indian peninsula, between Kerala to the south and Goa to the north, is the State of Karnataka, whose official language is Kannada. The State has always been addicted to films. With around a hundred cinemas for a population of two and a half million people, the State capital, Bangalore, is rated as one of the major film centres in India. But the films screened were principally in other South Indian languages or in Hindi or English. Kannada cinema made little progress till the 1970s. *Samskara* (Funeral Rites) dramatically brought Kannada films to the limelight, by being declared the Best Film of 1970. This was followed by a succession of very good (and award winning) Kannada films, which proved that *Samskara* was no flash in the pan. Through the seventies, each new year threw up at least one talented new director. One of the latest of these is Girish Kasaravalli, who won the President's Golden Lotus Award at 28, with his first film *Ghatashraddha* (The Ritual).

Born and brought up in Kasaravalli, a village in the Malnad (hill country) areas of Karnataka, his early exposure to films was limited to an occasional touring cinema. Finishing school in the district-headquarters' town of Shimoga, Girish went on to study pharmacology, and dreamt of discovering new drugs to cure malaria or medicines extracted from rare wild herbs, both of which are found in abundance in the Malnad.

His first encounters with film making were accidental. When on a visit to relatives in Heggodu (a little village which has found a permanent place in the annals of world cinema, because of pioneering experiments with rural audiences), Girish first came across some of the standard literature of films and film making. Later, while undergoing practical training with the Indian Drugs and Pharmaceuticals Limited in Hyderabad, he got to see some of the films of Satyajit Ray and Mrinal Sen. But though he encountered films late, it did not take him long to decide that this was the career for him.

In 1972, soon after completing his course in pharmacology, Girish joined the Film and Television Institute of India (FTII) in Pune, and registered for a Diploma in Film Direction. He feels that the course was enormously useful: "The Institute helped me a lot ... to see films ... analyse them ... and learn about film making techniques. One might know a lot about the aesthetics of cinema. But the FTII course provides a foundation in film technique." While at the Institute, his diploma film *Avashesh* (The Remnant) was declared the Best Student Film of 1975, and also went on to win the National Award for Best Experimental Short Film of that year. However, the diploma script which he submitted was not approved by the FTII jury. As he was not prepared to do an alternate script, he was not awarded his diploma. Ironically, this was the

101

same script from which he later shot *Ghatashraddha*.

As a person, Girish is totally absorbed in films and film making. His other interests are Kannada literature and theatre. He is currently the Principal of the Adarsh Film Institute, which conducts a one-year course to train film actors. As you enter the old house in which the Institute is located, the first thing that catches your eye is a series of stills from *Ghatashraddha* and from Satyajit Ray's *Pather Panchali* (Song of the Road). At first sight they could be mistaken for stills from the same film. Critics have often commented on similarities between Kasaravalli's and Ray's films; and therefore concluded that Girish Kasaravalli has been greatly influenced by Ray as a film maker. Girish himself denies this, though he admires much of Ray's work, and admits that the early Ray films contributed to his decision to become a director. But he accepts that the comparison is inevitable, since he has also chosen to make realistic films in b&w, with a strong emphasis on character, environment and motivation.

There are also similarities in their approach to film making. Girish prefers to work out a total script in advance, down to details of setting, props, action and camera movement. He prefers to keep improvisation to a minimum, though this is not always possible, because of constraints of time and money. His favourite directors are Bergman, Ozu and Antonioni. "I know this is a strange combination," he quickly adds. "And don't ask me why I like them or how they have influenced me. As a film maker, one does tend to appreciate the work of some directors more. It's like that."

Girish is married to Vaishali, the Kannada film and stage actress. They have a one-year-old son, Apurva.

While he is clear that he would like to continue making films as a career, he is a little concerned about the future of New Wave films in Kannada. The main problem is one of getting films screened for large audiences, and relevant audiences at that. For instance, he strongly feels that *Ghatashraddha,* which had a fairly successful run in Bangalore (and at film festivals and film societies at home and abroad) would have been most useful to the people of Malnad, who are its principal characters. But screening of films like this in rural areas is seen as too much of a commercial risk by distributors.

Last year, Girish joined with a group of people interested in promoting New Wave films to form the Navya Film Co-operative, which aimed at setting up a chain of theatres intended mainly for screening non-commercial films. But the experiment didn't pick up.

Girish is not sure what the answer to the problem will be, but he keeps trying. A shy and somewhat introspective person, he has also taken to writing, and is currently doing a series of articles on cinema for popular Kannada magazines.

Peter Colaco

GHATASHRADDHA
(The Ritual)

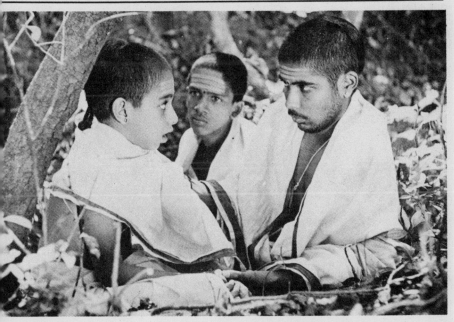

Nani (left), the new pupil, being bullied into submission by the older students

1977/B&W/144 mins/Kannada
Direction/Screenplay
Girish Kasaravalli
Produced by
Sadanand Suvarna
Story
Dr. U. R. Ananthamurthy
Camera
S. Ramachandra
Music
B. V. Karanth
Art Direction
K. V. Subanna
Editing
Umesh Kulkarni
Players
Ajit Kumar (Nani), Meena (Yamuna), Ramaswami Iyengar (Udupa), Shanta (Godavaramma), Jagannath (Sastri), Suresh (Ganesha)
Enquiries
Suvarnagiri Films, 6 Sheriar Baugh, Ramchandra Bhatt Marg, Bombay 400 009 Tel: 865490/861754

This is the story of a young widow who has transgressed the rigid sexual code of the orthodox brahmin society. The style is deceptively simple but is seeded with rich metaphor.

Yamuna is a child widow, living with her widowed father Udupa, a respected scholar who runs a *vedic* (ecclesiastical) school to which a young boy, Nani, is brought by his father as a live-in student. Yamuna's immediate sympathy for the lonely homesick boy turns into a bond of deep affection, nurtured by her thwarted maternity.

Yamuna is pregnant. She has been seduced by the teacher of the local government school. Already, the village gossip, Godavaramma, herself a widow, is agog with curiosity. She tries to get information out of Sastri, the older orphan student living at Udupa's house, as well as from the innocent Nani. Sastri hates the village and the study of Sanskrit. He plays truant when Udupa goes to the spiritual guru of his sect to seek financial help. Sastri smokes and gambles, steals money and takes sadistic pleasure in tormenting Nani, trying to wean him away from Yamuna.

Yamuna tries the medicines to induce abortion brought by her panicky lover, but none of them work. The boys led by Sastri, eavesdrop on their meeting in the forest. Nani

The Ritual, **highly
interesting in its subject
matter and beautifully
realised, was a fine
contribution to our
programme. The subtle
direction, the excellent
acting of all protagonists
and evocative rich B&W
photography, all came in
for praise and the film
was warmly clapped at
its conclusion.**

Erwin Rado, **Director
1979 Melbourne Film
Festival**

still does not understand what is happening but he is
slowly becoming aware and is ready to protect Yamuna.
By now, Godavaramma has spread the news of Yamuna's
pregnancy all over the village. Ganesha, the other resident
pupil at Udupa's school, is taken away by his father.
Sastri, too, leaves the house and tries to take Nani away
with him. But Nani remains with Yamuna after an initial
frightened attempt to leave, tenderly attending to her when
she faints.

Yamuna tries to commit suicide by going to the forest
and putting her arm down a snake-hole. She is rescued
by a terrified Nani, braving the forest late at night with
the help of an Untouchable worker.

Nani accompanies her to Parbu's house where his wife
is ready to perform a crude abortion. The schoolteacher
quietly slips out of the village while the abortion is under
way. In a powerful sequence weaving together the uncom-
prehending fear of the boy and the agony of Yamuna to
the drum-beats of drunkards dancing wildly, the abortion
is shown in all its cruelty.

The entire village is searching for Yamuna and Nani
and locate the two in the woods. Nani is wrenched away
from a drained Yamuna, wracked with pain and bereft of
hope. Her father, summoned home, is seen performing the
funeral rites for his yet living daughter.

The earthen pot, a symbol of fertility is broken, in a
negation of life. Yamuna is now dead to her father
and her community. She is last seen, her head clean-
shaven (as orthodox brahmin widows still are in parts
of South India), an outcaste discarded by society.

The film closes with the suggestion of a marriage
proposal for the widowed Udupa. The brahmin father
seen at the beginning, searching for a suitable bridegroom
for his daughter, is ready to offer his sixteen-year-old
girl to a man in his fifties. A candidate for another
Ghatashraddha, the director seems to ask, as the unaware, youthful girl appears in all her innocence.

*The erring young widow,
Yamuna, knowing that her
day of judgement is at hand.*

The film is set in the South India of the twenties. The ritual it describes is not practised now but the rejection of young widows by society continues.

Implicit in the film is the gradual erosion of respect for traditional learning of Sanskrit scriptures which only offered priesthood as a career. The visuals are replete with circular motifs. In Tantric philosophy, the circle signifies the womb.

Maithili Rao

Filmography

1975 AVASHESH (The Remnant)
Student documentary/B&W/20 mins
A short film made by Kasaravalli that won the Best Student Film Award at FTII. He uses a collage of images to question the validity of rituals surviving as anachronistic relics. It is conveyed through the enquiring eyes of a young boy, living in an old house, as he watches the annual rites for the dead.

1977 GHATASHRADDHA (The Ritual)

1979 AKRAMANA (The Siege)
Col/141 mins/Kannada
Lead Players: Vijaya Kashi, Vaishali Kasaravalli

Kasaravalli continues to be concerned with the constraints that chain women to their traditional roles. A romantic post-graduate student, living in a crowded old house with many interesting tenants, is intrigued by an attractive, older woman living with a small boy and no sign of a husband on the horizon. They fall in love, share their deepest thoughts, but in the end, the woman opts for her husband and the claims of motherhood. Disheartened but not defeated, the protagonist, now a college lecturer, embarks on a promising relationship with a student. The young girl and her widowed mother are under the strange dominance of her brother-in-law. She too deserts him. The siege ends in disillusionment.

1980 MOORU DARIGALU (The Three Paths)
Col/120 mins/Kannada
Lead Players: Sri Ranga, Vishwanath Rao

The latest film by Kasaravalli is his strongest indictment of the exploitation of women. Nirmala, a young adolescent girl, is the victim of malicious, unfounded gossip. Her father, a stern traditionalist, hurriedly arranges a marriage for her. The idealistic school-master who agrees to the marriage has lofty ideas that evade reality. No one has bothered to find out the truth about the alleged incident involving her with a photographer in the city. Wilful, almost obstinate, the girl commits suicide, not as an admission of defeat but as the only gesture of protest open to her.

AWTAR KAUL

It is difficult to evaluate the work of a person who has left behind only one film. Reviews of course are a transitory thing. But one feels happy when 'Sight & Sound' praises *27 Down's* intelligent use of locations. True, Kaul displays a mature style in his first film. One can gauge what could have been in his mind when one remembers that his greatest sorrow was that he could not get a film to make for the National Film Board of Canada.

Many artists achieve recognition only after death. Awtar Kaul may be said to have joined this group in a small way.

One's mind goes back to that fateful evening of July 20, 1974. At the usual Bombay coffee-shop rendezvous of young film makers. Awtar Kaul was wondering how to raise his passage money to Locarno, where his first feature film *27 Down* was entered as India's official entry. But by night the same day, he was dead, drowned while trying to rescue a friend — a young woman journalist.

Ironically, the news bulletin of the same night carried news of the National Film Awards. Kaul's film had won two honours: Best Hindi Film and Best B&W Photography. He had died probably without even hearing the news bulletin.

For young Indian film makers who wished to break away from the escapist commercial cinema, the early seventies were the years when revolution in attitudes was round the corner. The Film Finance Corporation, a government financing body which had been in existence for some years, had suddenly woken up to the fact that there was young talent in the country and had started giving small loans (Rs. 3 to 5 lakhs or $ 51,000) to technically qualified persons who produced a good script.

It was, therefore, not unusual to find young hopefuls scurrying about with sheaves of paper which contained their notion of cinema. But the ones to make the most use of these were the students of the FTII, the largest film school in Asia.

This was the heady atmosphere of the early seventies. Although he was not one of them, it was possible to see Awtar Kaul with other young hopefuls from the Film Institute, animatedly discussing films or laughing at the inanities of the commercial cinema. Quite a few of this crowd had already applied for the Film Finance Corporation loan. Kaul had himself submitted his script for the film *27 Down* (The Benares Express) based on a story by the Hindi writer Ramesh Bakshi.

A thickset strapping man, Kaul would appear to be brooding most of the time. He had an ugly temper when provoked but otherwise was the strong, silent kind. He had immense physical strength and energy and he drove himself mercilessly when shooting his film. *27 Down* was shot mostly in stations, running trains and railway yards. Many a time he and his cameraman A. K. Bir escaped death on the tracks because of Kaul's strength and quickness. For difficult top-angle shots, for instance, he would clamber aboard a pillar and support Bir and the camera on his shoulder. Even before succumbing to death, he swam the heavy rain-lashed seas for almost half a mile.

Awtar Kaul had graduated in film direction from the City University of New York. He would often narrate humorous tales about himself in New York. After his return to Bombay, he was a constant visitor at the newspaper offices where this writer worked. One day he suddenly remarked that the din of the teleprinters reminded him of the Associated Press. When in America, to support himself, he had taken up the job of copyholder with AP. One fine day, Kaul was caught by the editor reading Arthur Koestler's 'Darkness at Noon' on the job. He felt quite sure of being fired promptly. The editor called the erring Indian and after assuring himself that the young man appeared well read, made him a newsbrief writer!

Coming back to India posed a great deal of problems for Kaul. He had left his American wife back there and in India was faced with uncertainties about finance and the general lack of opportunities for a creative person. Nevertheless he stuck it out, doing no other job except to assist in the Ivory/Merchant film *Bombay Talkie*.

But once his loan was sanctioned, he started with all his zeal and energy as if he knew that this was to be his only film. In terms of philosophy of the cinema, Kaul was no dogmatist. He would defend the most abstract of treatments as well as the simplest. But for himself, cinema meant the simplest and most honest way to communicate with his audience. He believed in every style. But for himself, communication was the keystone on which a film made it or didn't make it. In those days, it had become a bit of a fashion to criticise Satyajit Ray. Most young film makers would unabashedly demolish Mr. Ray and set up their own cult figure: Ritwik Ghatak, another Bengali film maker and a contemporary of Mr. Ray.

But Awtar Kaul sensibly steered clear of these ideologies. He had yet to make his film and that would say all he had to. In fact, Satyajit Ray's *Jalsaghar* (Music Room) was one of his favourites. He had lost count of the number of times he had seen it.

Unfortunately, various factors not only delayed his film but threatened to push his budget overboard. The Benares sequences were very difficult. Equipment wouldn't reach them in time. Kaul would often, out of frustration, fashion trolleys out of handcarts. He was also running an ugly temperature. To top it all, his heroine was a temperamental star of the Bombay screen. He dealt with them all with quiet efficiency and humour. Once when Raakhee, his actress, insisted that her shots be taken because she had given him the dates, Kaul sardonically remarked that during that particular period he found trees much more fascinating than Raakhee. The star couldn't help laughing.

Once *27 Down* was completed, Kaul set about trying to find buyers. He knew how chary distributors are of touching a B&W film. The Indian distribution system does not allow even limited shows for low budget films, calling them experimental and obscurantist. At his death, his wife, family and cameraman, A. K. Bir, were left with the responsibility of his debts and the distribution of the film.

Mercifully, *27 Down* had a very successful run in Bombay four years after it was completed.

J. S. Rao

27 DOWN

anjay, hopelessly adrift, finds companionship for a while in the working woman Shalini.

973/B&W/118 mins/Hindi
Direction/Produced by/
Screenplay
Awtar Krishna Kaul
Story
Ramesh Bakshi
Camera
A. K. Bir
Editing
Ravi Patnaik
Music
Bhuben Hari
Art Direction
Bansi Chandragupta
Players
Raakhee (Shalini), M. K. Raina
(Sanjay), Rekha Sabnis
(Sanjay's wife), Om Shivpuri
(Sanjay's father)
Enquiries
National Film Development
Corporation,
13-16 Regal Chambers,
Nariman Point,
Bombay 400 021
Tel: 232183/232218

27 Down suggests a feeling of desolation, the emptiness that follows a period of intense happiness. Like a train disappearing into the dusk, leading nowhere. The film has the dark foreboding of an approaching tunnel.

In relating the train to the inevitability of one's life, the director traces the mind of a troubled, sensitive and cynical young man, Sanjay. His life is lived literally on a train. Since childhood he has been in awe of his father, who was an engine driver (an accident forced him to retire prematurely).

Sanjay grows up. He opts for art school. His love for trains has worn off but not the fear of his father. Father and fate conspire to get him back on the right track — the railway ones.

He is inducted into the secure, claustrophobic life of the railways. Despite Sanjay's protests, the father decides that "facilities" like free travel and housing are not to be disregarded. Leaving art school, Sanjay becomes a ticket inspector on a train.

Whatever hopes and ambitions Sanjay might have had are soon forgotten. He is swallowed up by the railways, engulfed in their sooty, choking grasp. His casual attire gives way to the anonymity of the ticket-inspector's uniform. The last traces of rebellion vanish. He has accepted the "system." Life falls into a rut, a monotonous pattern.

Fate intervenes in the form of a beautiful commuter, Shalini, a stenographer working with the Life Insurance Corporation (a symbolic job, one presumes). There is instant empathy between the two lonely people. Their love blossoms in railway compartments, refreshment rooms, beaches and her bed-sitter apartment. For Sanjay life gains a purpose, a sense of anticipation and excitement. Even the monotony of train journeys is now tinged with nostalgia.

The brief encounter is destined only to be a respite. The father decides it is time to put an end to his son' "indiscretions." He recalls him on a pretext of illness. The boy is summarily married off to a rich shrew who is saving her virginity for the wedding night. She explodes the myth of the shy, modest village belle and hurls herself on the dispirited groom. Her dowry includes, besides cash and furnishings, four buffaloes and an old, illiterate father. The wife chatters incessantly, stupidly, going on at him about his earlier romance. Sanjay is increasingly repulsed by her crassness.

A chance encounter with Shalini makes him realise his loss. What has made him behave so irrationally, he asks himself. The claustrophobia is stifling. He has to get away from it all.

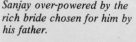
Sanjay over-powered by the rich bride chosen for him by his father.

He takes the "27 Down" train to Benares. Any place is good enough. He finds a sense of release. The booze, the whores, the hills, all assist in his introspection.

The working woman, Shalini, who questions Sanjay's acquiescence. 27 Down is one of the earliest of the new films in which a film star of the calibre of Raakhee plays a lead role.

He tries to discover the meaning of life. For a while he believes that life will take a new direction. But, seemingly without will, he returns to his destination ... back to his wife, the buffaloes, the stench, the father-in-law.

In desperation Sanjay seeks out Shalini. It is hopeless. She is not the same person any more. She reacts coldly, without any feeling. He persists. Can the past return? Why don't they try and work something out? They plan a meeting, which does not materialise.

He is tired, exhausted by constant movement leading to nothing. He wants to rest now, to let his senses drift into numbness. He moves back into nothingness.

About a young man who is forced by an injury to his engine-driver father to join the railways instead of studying art, it makes wonderfully imaginative use of trains, tracks and aimless journeys that echo his despair. A little too long, a little too self-indulgent, it is nevertheless a strikingly intelligent piece of work.

Tom Milne
The Observer (U.K.)
May 25, 1975

27 Down was one of the earliest films of the new school to deal with a deadening exactness, on the alienation of the urban mind. Somehow Awtar Kaul mirrored the feelings of his generation caught between rural mores and city needs, between inner aspirations and forced ambitions, between wanting a liberated life partner and settling for a pre-arranged spouse. The film was made eight years ago. Its sorrowing negation of self and soul holds true even now.

MANI KAUL

Mani Kaul has physical substance, an easy expansiveness and confidence that is striking. He has hands that hold a gesture firmly.

He has a resonant voice which he uses in his films, in his exploration of the essence of *raagas* (melodies) in Indian classical music, in subtly inflected statements about his work.

Mani is articulate about his work which has been little viewed and even less appreciated in the country of its origin, though winning critical acclaim. Yet, such is his creative vitality that, in an environment that is at best ignorant and at worst hostile, he has made, in the 14 years since his graduation from Pune's Film Institute, nine films.

The crackle of leather shoes on a windswept hill, the brash red and white of a desert city, the bend of a neck and lift of an eye, the inward turned gaze of human beings, these are the sensuous impressions through which Mani's films work. The influence of Bresson is evident. Writing about his latest film, he quotes Bresson to illustrate what he had tried to do: "Bring together things that have as yet never been brought together and did not seem predisposed to be so." But whereas Bresson relates his work to a larger framework of belief, Mani rejects all such frameworks.

"All the work that I have seen or read that has been created from within an ideology," he says, "has been purely illustrative. Such work is not strictly artistic." At the same time he grants true artistic value to the works of Bresson, Tarkovsky and Muktibodh, the Hindi writer. About Muktibodh's writings he says, "His Marxism permeates his work because it is a total philosophy. His work is a dialectical struggle between word and emotion."

Eschewing ideology, narrative and emotion, eschewing psychology and character, Mani sets out to discover, heuristically, what may be revealed in the film, by the film. He begins with no axioms: "Artistic activity does not lie in deciphering the sensuousness that people experience, but in reaching a new sensuousness through each film."

At the beginning of a film, the only thing that Mani knows positively is what he does *not* want to do. What he wants to do is revealed to him as the work proceeds. "If you begin with an idea," he says, "you are trapped into illustrating it and thus limiting it. Actually, every film should have the potential to spark off a hundred ideas."

Over the years Mani has worked towards greater freedom from such constraints as script and predecided length. In his last film he achieved his ideal of having no script at all to work from, nor sketched frames, nor pre-planned camera positions. He did what a good Indian classical musician would do. He improvised.

Classical Indian music is to Mani the purest artistic search. The *alaap* or slow unfolding of a *raaga* (melody) to get its innermost *swaroop* (form), is its finest expression. Just as a good musician has mastered the musical method of construction which saves his delineation of a *raag* from becoming formless, so a good film maker has a firm control over cinematic methods of construction and can therefore allow himself to improvise.

Watching Mani's films with their attenuated moments of time, their slow and measured gestures and the staccato rhythm of voices drained of all emotion, one experiences a suspension of time. This is the principle of displacement in operation. Mani quotes a ninth century Sanskrit text by Ananda Vardhan called 'Dhwanyalok' where this principle is enunciated as forming the basis of all art. Unless an image displaces itself from its natural state, it acquires no significance. Displacement causes resonance. Again Mani turns to Indian classical music to illustrate the point. "The full notes of the octave have their conventional, mathematical positions. The *shrutis* or half and quarter notes have no absolute positions. The same *shruti* slides a little this way or that to form endlessly varied relationships with other notes."

The principle of displacement works in discovering the specificity of objects. Displacement enhances the actual existence of object and immediately illuminates it. "Performance in cinema," says Mani, "is internalisation. After displacement, this is the second great law. The player must consider his own reality juxtaposed against the text, and remove from his mind the convention of presenting himself as another person. Without turning into a recitation of the text, the process must acquire the strength of an encounter with the text. Just as a painter works with paints on a finite surface, so also the actor must work with words and objects in real and existing spaces and not become a character. Like music retires now and then into silence, the actor must retire into himself."

"That is all very well," an actor on the sets of *Ashad ka ek Din* (A Monsoon Day) is supposed to have said. "Our gestures must be controlled. But here we see life as full of drama." The reference was to the flamboyant gestures with which Mani was directing. It is the same flamboyance that he brings to the classroom, evoking in his students a highly charged response. And the same flamboyance with which he holds a group of young film makers, gathered around him, in awed attention. Not surprisingly, Mani enjoyed acting in his Film Institute days, "mainly because the direction classes were extremely boring." He appeared in many student exercises while he was there. He also had a role in Basu Chatterji's first film, *Sara Akash* (The Whole Sky).

Besides being a film maker, Mani is an avid painter ever since 1970. In 1975 he held a one-man show in Bombay. Prior to that, one of his paintings was sold in a collective effort to raise funds for Bangladesh refugees. The National Museum of Modern Art in New Delhi has a Mani Kaul painting on exhibit. He describes his style as abstract.

Shanta Gokhale

Mani Kaul is soft-spoken and informal but given to violent reaction when upset. People have learnt to tread warily with him in argument. Otherwise, Mani has a surprisingly quick and animated sense of humour and loves cracking jokes at himself. For his latest (and most obscure) film when it was in competition in the Eighth International Film Festival in New Delhi, he says in great glee that he stood outside the empty hall offering his ten free passes to unsuspecting pedestrians, who when they heard his name, fled in the opposite direction.

USKI ROTI
(A Day's Bread)

The contrite wife waits for hours to give her husband (a bus driver) his mid-day meal.

1970/B&W/110 mins/Hindi
Direction/Script
Mani Kaul
Produced by
Rochak Pandit
Camera
K. K. Mahajan
Editing
Hemanta Bose
Players
Gurdeep Singh (Sucha Singh),
Garima (Balo),
Enquiries
National Film Development
Corporation,
3/16 Regent Chambers,
Nariman Point,
Bombay 400 021.
Phone: 232183/232218

At a desolate bus stop on a highway, set against a barren landscape in the plains of Punjab, is the figure of a village woman — Balo. She waits . . . and waits.

Each afternoon she walks two miles from her village to the bus stop to deliver the mid-day meal to her husband Sucha Singh — a Sikh bus driver who expects his wife to perform, without a murmur, the traditional duties of the average Indian rural housewife: a lifelong drudge, hopeless fatalist, little more than a beast of burden. As for Sucha Singh himself, daily shuttling between Nakodar and Jullundur — the two termini of his route — he has time to visit her only once a week, on Tuesday. The rest of the week, he has his fellow bus drivers, his drinking and card-playing sessions. And, of course, the wavy-haired mistress in Nakodar as an extra diversion.

Balo accepts it all. Tradition has trained her to find alibis for him. Doesn't he, after all, give her fifty rupees every month to run the house? He could, if he wanted, stop coming home even on that one day in the week. And what man hasn't his special needs, his exclusive expenses?

On this particular day, as she waits there at the bus stop, she has missed the bus timing. She arrived when Sucha Singh had already driven off. Back in the village, 14-year-old Jinda, her younger sister and only companion, was nearly seduced by Jangi, the village rake. Balo tries to restore the frightened girl's courage but the incident

115

has filled her own mind with confusion. Hidden fears about the insecurity of her life creep in. Knowing well that she will not reach the bus stop on time, she has dutifully made the journey, like a ritual done in a trance. And Balo waits there at the bus stop with the carefully wrapped meal nursed in her hand.

Later during the day the bus arrives. And now Sucha Singh, in a foul temper, refuses to accept the meal. She attempts to explain and plead. But the bus storms away trailed by swirling dust. A threat hangs in the air that Sucha Singh will never forgive Balo for the lapse

Crushed and wounded, Balo still feels guilty. If only she had pleaded with him a little more . . .

Now, it will be night before he brings back the last bus She decides to go on waiting. By sundown, she is alone Alone with herself.

During this superficially calm span of a few hours spent in waiting, memories, fears, fantasies and reveries swirl in Balo's feverish mind blurring the line between physical reality and mental vision . . . what if Sucha decides to leave her? Does he really have a mistress? If he came to know about Jaggi's advances towards Jinda, won't he beat him up? Maybe back at home Jaggi has forced Jinda into submission. What of that bleak, misty morning when they all went to recover the body of Loto Singh's wife who, deserted by her husband, had committed suicide by drowning.

A storm surrounds the bus stop . . . Balo's feet bleed

A gentle hand touches Balo's shoulders. Sucha Singh uncomfortable at having to display affection, reveals he has been moved by her devotion. Balo has succeeded in conveying to him the meaning of their relationship.

Sucha Singh accepts the meal packet and promises to return to her the following Tuesday. He asks what she had to say in the afternoon.

For Balo, that can wait. The bus rattles away into the darkness. Balo is once again surrounded by the stillness of the night.

Uski Roti **is a bitter story of loneliness underlined by slow gestures and simple words in a traditional ritual atmosphere. Past, present and future mingle in one time, which is itself timeless. It attempts to solve the old contradiction between a simple and impressionistic cinematic language. The narrative proceeds very slowly with a crude reality and yet so evanescent in its bitterness of unspoken words.**

Avvenuire **commenting on the film when it was entered at the 32nd Venice Film Festival, 1972.**

Filmography

1966 **YATRIK (The Traveller)**
(Student documentary) Col/20 mins
It concerns two young couples on a visit to the Ajanta caves. The film observes their interaction thereby weaving subtle character studies on a personal key.

1969 **USKI ROTI (A Day's Bread)**

1971 **ASHAD KA EK DIN (A Monsoon Day)**
B&W/143 mins/Hindi
Lead players: Rekha Sabnis, Arun Khopkar, Om Shivpuri S. N. Dhir
A literary film based on a play in three acts. It portrays the love of Mallika and Kalidasa, the renowned Sanskrit

poet and dramatist. Vilom, friend to both and interested in Mallika is a passive onlooker for the first two acts. Kalidasa leaves his mountain-valley verdant home for the splendour of far off Ujjain where he wins fame. The action is rooted in the village to which Kalidasa returns years later and finds Mallika married to Vilom and the mother of his child. Mallika sacrifices her love so that the poet could pursue his muse.

1973   **DUVIDHA (In Two Minds)**
Col/82 mins/Hindi
Lead players: Ravi Menon, Raisa Padamsee, Hardan, Shambudan

The story works at the mythic level of a ghost who falls in love with a new bride. He takes the place of the absent husband who is away on business. In time, the woman has borne the ghost a child and the real husband is summoned home. A wise shepherd captures the ghost but the woman pines for the ghostly lover.

The first three feature films focus in an individual way on the condition of woman in a tradition bound society.

1974   **THE NOMAD PUPPETEERS** (documentary)
Col/18 mins
The film portrays the life and art of the traditional puppeteers of Rajasthan. It also shows how modern life has affected them.

1977   **CHITRAKATHI** (documentary)
Col/18 mins
It depicts the folk artists of Konkan in Maharashtra who narrate religious stories with the help of leather puppets.

1980   **ARRIVAL** (documentary)
Col/20 mins
A candid study of the bustling metropolis of Bombay and the faceless crowds that constitute its labour force.

1980   **SATAH SE UTHATA AADMI**
(Rising from the Surface)
Col/144 mins/Hindi
Lead players: Gopi, M. K. Raina, Vibhuti Jha

The film has no formal plot and is based on the text of one of the greatest Hindi writers. Three main players represent three divergent ideas. It moves from individual struggle to those involving social classes. The entire film is a conscious negation of the technique of montage and each shot is complete in itself to give a feeling of time unfolding and create its own movement.

KETAN MEHTA

Ketan Mehta says: "While I was in college, I was active in street-theatre. From college, we would go out on the road, into 'jhuggies' (slums) and put up instant, one-act plays against imperialism. At the Film Institute, I realised all cinema is political—it either wants change or cunningly maintains the status quo. Every film reflects the ideology of its director, whether he supports justice or evil."

Ketan Mehta's film was being shown to a film society crowd. When Ketan climbed onto the dais, a man sitting next to me remarked, "I think the director couldn't make it." He could not believe that the man before us, 5' 3" and seemingly 23 years old (but in fact 29) was the director . . . .

Ketan was doing a student film at FTII. He asked his cameraman how many shots he would like to take in a shift. The cameraman felt that 25 was a comfortable number. Ketan said, "Excellent. I've planned only 60." He finished five minutes before time . . . .

After his FTII diploma, Ketan was working on SITE (Satellite Instructional Television Experiment) as a TV producer. He was assigned a program series on local problems. He went out with a ½" portable video-camera, stayed with the Untouchables, prepared his script and got the fiercely shy or resentful villagers to act for him. He had just one assistant and shot the footage himself. The programs lacked the polish of a professional TV presentation. But the impact was tremendous. The upper-caste Hindus threatened to stone the community TV sets and to boycott the organization. This was his first experience of rural India. It affected him deeply as an artist and as a person; and contained the seed of his first film on the Untouchables.

Ketan's working for TV in Ahmedabad led to another important event in his personal life. There he met Archana his lovely wife, who was studying textiles at the National Institute of Design. The exquisite costumes of *Bhavni Bhavai* (A Folk Tale) have been designed by her. The vitality of their relationship flows from shared interests.

Theatre was Ketan's first passion. In his college days, he was associated with a group called *Dishantar,* which had in it many notable theatre personalities. Ketan felt unhappy with the elitist nature of the group. By this time he had become interested in radical politics.

His first encounter with the writings of Bertolt Brecht was a turning point. He joined a street-theatre group with actor M.K. Raina and directed two plays of Brecht, 'Exception and the Rule' and 'In Search of Justice'. They were politically aware without being affiliated to any party. It meant discovering theatre, discovering oneself, working very hard and above all enjoying it.

In theatre, Ketan tried his hand at acting, set-designing, lighting, costumes and direction. Apart from the technical knowledge he gained, it helped him to relate to people through group activity. His experiences on both sides of the footlights made it easy for his actors and technicians to work with him.

A true joyfulness, zaniness, naughtiness is a rare thing in Indian cinema. The humour of the commercial cinema is laboured, never spontaneous. A good, healthy laugh is rare. It is even more rare in serious Indian cinema. *Bhavni Bhavai* has some really funny moments. Ketan loves the comic-strip form, and is an admirer of Goscinny and Uderzo. What fascinates him is the crystalline quality of their visuals. They do not duplicate the dialogue, but create an audio-visual image. He uses the technique of animation through gestures and movement of character to derive the final positions of expression.

Meyerhold quoting Pushkin says that laughter, pity and terror are the three strings of our imagination that vibrate to the impact of drama. In Chaplin, laughter and pity take over whilst terror remains muted. In Eisenstein, pity and terror predominate.

Chaplin and Eisenstein have had a major cinematic influence on Ketan. In his first film he dealt with pity and laughter. In his second film, he is planning to deal with terror and pity.

His work on TV newsreel coverage, combined with his experience of street theatre, made him aware of one of the most important problems facing an Indian film maker. The *cinema verite* programs he made initially with the Untouchables presented only the surface of their reality. It is only when he attempted stylisation with folk forms that the programs became relevant.

His TV work included children's programs which he enjoyed tremendously. Although the programs were educational, they were full of fun. The fun wasn't an extraneous element that sugarcoated a "message". The message itself was alive with the joy of life. Again he was able to mix preoccupations and experiment freely.

The most valuable part of Ketan's TV work was watching his programs with a rural audience. It can be a brutal experience when your message is misunderstood; your best gags don't come off and the laugh is at your expense. It teaches you to be objective about your work. The other points of view are just forced upon you. Assimilating them is painful but rewarding. Ketan feels that the boundaries between theatre, TV and film are not rigid. He tends to fuse these media in his work. His only *bete noire* is neo-realism. At its best, he finds it a predictable and dull form. At its worst, trivial. He feels that neo-realism is incapable of dealing with the essence. This is a lesson he has learnt from his masters: Eisenstein, Brecht, Chaplin, Bunuel, and the great Indian director Ritwik Ghatak.

There is a restlessness and impatience in Ketan which makes him seek a quick solution in his creative work. Many times it works brilliantly, but at others, it becomes a convenient shortcut. Perhaps it is necessary for him to come to terms with himself. There is ample evidence of bold innovation, joyous creativity, a lot of cool courage and spunk.

The director studied at Poona and financed his film through the formation of a cooperative with other graduates. The costumes by Archana Shah are stunning; songs and dances are both entertaining and "in situation." Mehta seemed the most perceptive and talented of the gaggle of young directors whose work was on show in Delhi.

Elliott Stein
Film Comment
July 1981

Arun Khopkar

BHAVNI BHAVAI
(A Folk Tale)

Colour/135 mins/1980/Gujarati
Direction/Screenplay
Ketan Mehta
Produced by
Sanchar Film Coop.
Society Ltd.
Camera
Krishnakant "Pummy"
Music
Gaurang Vyas
Art Direction
Mira Lakhia
Editing
Ramesh Asher
Players
Naseeruddin Shah (the king),
Smita Patil (Ujaan),
Mohan Gokhale (Jivo),
Om Puri (Malo),
Dina Pathak (Dhuli),
Suhasini Mulay
(younger queen),
Benjamin Gilani
(Commander-in-Chief,
Nimesh Desai (Ranglo)
Gopi Desai (Rangli)
Enquiries
Sanchar Film Co-operative
Society,
Nehru Foundation,
Thaltej Tekra, Vastrapur Road,
Ahmedabad-380 058.
Tel: 442642.

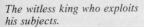
The witless king who exploits his subjects.

The *Bhavai*, a dying form of folk drama in Gujarat, synthesizes diverse arts into socially relevant communication. The film is based on one such ancient *Bhavai* tale called 'Achhootno Vesh' (Garb of the Untouchable) which tells of the exploitation of Harijans (so low in the caste hierarchy that they were considered Untouchable). In this particular region the upper castes enforced restrictions of dress that marked as well as dehumanized the Harijans. Thus, the Harijan had to wear a broom behind him to erase his offensive footprints; he was required to don a third sleeve as a sign of submission; he had to carry a clay spittoon around his neck; and he could only wear unwoven yarn as head-dress.

The screenplay is by Ketan Mehta and it shows a

121

spirited and highly individual approach to its subject matter. The problem of caste is a delicate and sensitive one in which people of all rank and file stand demeaned and accused. The camera in fact accuses the audience of permitting cruelty and exploitation to continue unresisted all around us.

Bhavni Bhavai tells its story on two levels. One is the present which deals with a poor Untouchable community whose huts have been burnt down and who are now desperate and homeless. A minstrel decides to revive their morale with a folk song. As he sings, the film goes into the past, enacting the song itself.

The song is a parody about a foolish king who has two wives but no heir. He and his courtiers exploit the Untouchables of the villlage. One of their many menial tasks is to clean the royal bathrooms. The palace is stinking because the Untouchables are away attending a wedding. They are hauled back and beaten to death for this offence.

The older queen gives birth to a son, to the chagrin of the younger queen. The latter conspires with her lover to have the baby killed. The courtiers relent and set the baby afloat in a box. The baby is found by a childless Untouchable couple.

The baby grows up into Jivo, a handsome and carefree youth. He falls in love with a spirited gypsy girl named Ujaan, who signifies the spirit of liberation. She

The gypsy girl, Ujaan who stands for the spirit of liberation.

A delightful didactic fable with sharp Brechtian influences that works on practically all levels. This colourful film is inventive in its costuming, playing, setting and imbuing a comedy parable with digestible statements on authoritarianism and revolt.

Gene Moskowitz,
Variety (U.S.A)
January 1981

Jivo, a brahmin brought up by Untouchables, gives his life for a cause.

chides him into discarding the demeaning aspects of an Untouchable's garb. She dares him to display his defiance in the town.

They run away together, Meanwhile, the younger queen discovers the secret of Jivo's identity. She bribes the astrologer to warn the king that a man called Jivo portends death for the king. Spurred on by Ujaan, Jivo strikes a bargain. He agrees to surrender if his people are allowed the dignity of normal attire.

The film has two endings. One, a happy fairy-tale reprieve; the other, a more disturbing one where Jivo is executed with tragic consequences for everyone.

The film moves back and forth between past and present. The same actors are identifiable in both. It tells its story through folk song, mime and dance.

Uma da Cunha

"The film is dedicated to Asait Thakore, who wrote the history of the Bhavai form in the 14th century. There are many legends about him, but one thing is certain, he was a brahmin, a great scholar and singer, excommunicated by his people.

The other dedication is to Bertolt Brecht. He studied the epic structure from Noh and Kabuki theatre. If he had come to India, he would have seen Bhavai is also an epic form and perhaps freer in its capacity to make a point than any other."

Ketan Mehta

Filmography

1975 MADHYA SURYA (The Midday Sun) (documentary)
B&W/26 mins
Through the story of a merchant who sets out in search of a hidden treasure, the film reveals how greed and fear can dehumanise a man.

COOLIES AT BOMBAY CENTRAL
B&W/35 mm/10 mins
A student film made at the Film Institute in Pune. As the the title suggests, it depicts the life of railway porters at a bustling Bombay terminus.

1977 EXPERIENCE INDIA
Col/16 mm
Made in collaboration with travel agencies, the film describes youth festivals and cultural shows in certain parts of India.

Ketan Mehta has also made a series of TV films called *Wat Amari* (In conversation) dealing with the problems of Untouchables and other sociological issues.

This year he plans to make two feature films. *Holi* (The Spring Festival) deals with the lives of college students living in hostels. The other film is titled *Raktabeej* (Seed of Blood).

SAEED MIRZA

If you were to ask Saeed Mirza an awkward question, he would probably fling an even more tricky one at you. A very difficult man to corner, Mirza is the most vociferous spokesman on the Parallel Cinema movement in India, Compact, with a straight no-nonsense beard. Saeed Mirza, in his mid-thirties, is still an angry young man.

"Middle class" is generally anathema to Saeed Mirza, and he conveys it in his work. To him, it is represented by the State and its inefficient bureaucracy, and also the false facade of morality that is prevalent everywhere. In both his feature films, he has tried to expose the class for the hypocrisy it harbours.

Right from the start, Mirza makes it clear that he is no watered-down socialist, getting across his leftist philosophy obliquely or subtly. He is direct, he hits at the audience, whether in a cinema hall or across the table. In fact, in his films he has rejected the standard narrative form precisely because it dilutes the impact of the social comment that he is making. "The form has lost its credibility," he says.

Of late, Mirza has been using a deliberate kind of pastiche to convey his ideas. However, in his first film, *Arvind Desai Ki Ajeeb Dastaan* (The Strange Tale of Arvind Desai) Mirza used a classical though non-narrative structure. The central character Desai, was, quite simply, Mirza himself, in a state of flux, as he puts it. The film was an "attempt at understanding the urban middle class, who are exposed to ideas, but reject them when it comes to the crunch, especially economic." Like Desai, Mirza was brought up on unquestioned values. But for him, when it came to the crunch, he held back and questioned, instead of succumbing. "Not that I passed the test of my own convictions," he says with a smile, "but at least I saw through the hypocrisy."

Mirza's cynicism about the society he lives in, although not of a very bitter kind, stems in part from his own experience. As far as his work goes, he has been fairly unlucky. The two documentary films which he made before renouncing the form, "because documentary being State controlled, has to project a certain view," were kept in the cans. The films — one, about the eviction of slum dwellers and the other, on problems of urban housing, were regarded as controversial. For Mirza, it is now a closed chapter, but he has not forgotten. *Arvind Desai* has also not yet had a theatrical release, because the National Film Development Corporation (NFDC) that financed the film did not, until recently, have an effective distribution and release set-up.

However, in *Albert Pinto Ko Gussa Kyon Aata Hai,* (What Makes Albert Pinto Angry) Mirza has evened the score. The film, set in an Indian Christian family, a culture that Mirza is familar with, being married to a Roman Catholic himself, has been applauded everywhere. "It's nice to be successful," grins Mirza. And with belated, inevitable cynicism, he adds wryly. "Now the critics will begin saying that I've gone commercial, that I've sold out." He continues, "My next film will convince them of it." Already scripted, the next venture is to explore the ethos of a five-star hotel, and predictably enough, it is titled *Five Star Hotel.*

He seems to have a penchant for unusual, expressive titles. A film planned for the future is going to have the impossible title *Mr. and Mrs. Joshi Go to Court for Justice.* "*Five Star Hotel* is to be a comedy," says Mirza with a mock-serious expression on his face, "and it will put my point across as forcefully as ever."

Mirza throws his own convictions at the audience throughout the film. "I want to keep at it," he says. So long as the logic of the film is intact, he believes that there is no harm in using characters and situations that are tangential to the plot but part of the ideology that he wishes to propagate. "I provide my own perceptions," he says frankly, and the audience can take it or leave it.

In Mirza's films, rarely is a character "established" in the conventional sense of the term. He is more the clothing for an idea. Mirza's fondest wish (and he becomes very serious as he talks of this) is to achieve a cinema of ideas, in the true sense, where you can rise above the characters and make your social comment without inhibition.

Because of this attitude, his work is often described as patchy, derivative and incoherent. To Mirza, this point of view is evidence of a pragmatism towards art and life, which he abhors. But generally speaking, he is the last person to avoid criticism. He subjects his own work to a harsh enough analysis. He admits that his future efforts will be more organised, his style more defined, in that it will strive for a form that is politically and historically relevant to the present context. "Each film is the take-off point for my next film," he explains, and that's how there is a distinct development in his style.

It is the mixed interpretations to his work in themselves that spell a kind of success to Mirza. "Nobody was indifferent to my film," he says with satisfaction. To him, planting an idea in the viewer's mind takes precedence over all else.

Mirza's openness to ideas manifests itself even in the way he works. The atmosphere during the making of a film is very casual, with "everybody throwing up suggestions," as he puts it. Although he has every shot defined before he starts shooting, he allows the actors a fair amount of freedom. "I let them improvise," he says, "so long as they do not misconstrue the basic premise of the film."

He finds that he has more and more to say. "And I will keep saying it," he says determinedly. Because he refuses to compromise. "I see around me a dehumanised world," he says with conviction. "It has a kind of morality that is extremely false. It represents a middle class fascism, which is the ruling idea, the ruling philosophy. All I'm trying to do is to question it." In other words, what Mirza is trying to do, and what many hope he will achieve on the basis of the promise that he holds out today, is to conduct his own little revolution — on celluloid.

What is certain is that Mirza is a talent very much to be reckoned with, now and in the future."

Derek Malcolm
Guardian (U.K.)
January 17, 1981

Rohini Nilekani

ALBERT PINTO KO GUSSA KYON AATA HAI
(What Makes Albert Pinto Angry)

Albert Pinto acts high and mighty while his girl-friend sulks and his mother worries.

1980/Col/160 mins/Hindi
Direction/Produced by/Story
Saeed Mirza
Screenplay
Kundan Shah, Saeed Mirza
Camera
Virendra Saini
Editing
Renu Saluja
Music
Bhaskar Chandavarkar
Art Direction
Jennifer Mirza
Players
Naseeruddin Shah
(Albert Pinto) Shabana Azmi
(Stella D'Costa), Smita Patil
(Joan Pinto), Dilip Dhawan
(Dominic Pinto), Sulabha
Deshpande (Mrs. Pinto),
Arvind Deshpande (Mr. Pinto)
Enquiries
Saeed Akhtar Mirza
Productions, 47 A Nair Road,
Bombay 400 008.
Phone: 896849

In a film as provocative as its title, Saeed Mirza creates the distinctive milieu of Roman Catholics from Goa, now settled in pockets of Bombay and conscious of their minority status in a polyglot society.

Mirza's protagonist is Albert Pinto, a flashy garage mechanic, naively convinced of his superiority to the other mechanics, because his patrons, the owners of luxury limousines, treat him as a friend. He drives their cars and derives vicarious pleasure from their lifestyle. His anger is mainly directed against his girlfriend, Stella, the typical city secretary, for wearing skirts and chatting up the garage hands in a friendly fashion. His younger brother Dominic, a guitar-strumming and petty-thieving drop-out, is the other target of Albert's bourgeois anger. His father is a textile worker, the mother a godfearing housewife. His lame sister is a salesgirl. There is a special rapport between the father and daughter. She silently understands and applauds his joining a crucial strike at the factory. She has a pitying contempt for her brothers.

Stella's boss makes overtures to her, which is resented by Albert. Stella herself is a pragmatist, unaffected by her drunken father and her brother's dream of migrating to Canada. Albert's unpardonable rudeness exasperates her

127

and there is a temporary rift between them, till a contrite Albert comes back seeking her forgiveness.

Albert's realisation of the underlying class conflict comes when his father is beaten up. The affronts to his personal dignity from rich people whom he considered friends, educate him. In a search for his personal and class identity, Albert Pinto finds plenty to fuel his anger. He even begins to sympathise with his father's opposition to those who exploit the working class.

Albert Pinto drops his fancy airs and mingles with his colleagues.

Filmography

1976 **CORPSES** (documentary)
B&W/19 mins
Based on a short story by Gopal Radgaonkar, it deals with the life of three young boys who live off the pickings of dead bodies. The film attempts to show that relationships are often dictated not by human values but a struggle for survival in a hostile environment.

SLUM EVICTION (documentary)
B&W/20 mins
Focuses on the protest of 72,000 people living in a distant Bombay suburb against their eviction by government authorities. The land was acquired for an extension of a government institution.

URBAN HOUSING (documentary)
B&W/20 mins

Made for an organization called BUILD (Bombay Urban Industrial League Development). The film focuses on the problems of housing in Bombay.

1978   **ARVIND DESAI KI AJEEB DASTAAN (The Strange Tale of Arvind Desai)**
Col/120 mins
Lead Players: Dilip Dhawan, Anjali Paigankar, Om Puri, Abha Dhulia, Shreeram Lagoo, Sulabha Deshpande.
The film is an ironical study of urban corruption: how money subverts every value in life. Arvind Desai is an ineffective liberal, tortured by a bad conscience but unable to do anything about it except seek solace from a leftist friend. He has a love-hate relationship with his self-confident father and is angry with his mother for her passivity. His favourite whore serves as a temporary solace. His petite secretary with whom he is involved is gradually reduced to a commodity. He tacitly agrees to an arranged marriage with a girl of his own class. Only death is the answer for such a confused, sensitive individual, a mass of self-contradictions.

ALBERT PINTO KO GUSSA KYON AATA HAI (What Makes Albert Pinto Angry) Hindi

GOVIND NIHALANI

The Indian government is co-producing the (*Gandhi*) film, guaranteeing more than 6.5 million dollars raised from private sources. The rest of the $22 million came from a U. S.—British investment group. Many Indian film makers wonder why such monies are not available to them, though, ironically, Nihalani, director of *Wounded*, was second unit director on *Gandhi*. He believes that if the film, which uses local players and technicians, is successful it will draw world attention to India.

Gene Moskowitz
Covering Indian entries in the Cannes Film Festival, International Herald Tribune (U.S.A.) May 23/24, 1981

Watching Nihalani work, one is aware of controlled tension. The camera becomes almost a weapon, so much an extension of his vision that one wonders where the technician and the man become separate beings. Without, I hope, giving offence to Govind Nihalani, I don't think they are.

As a cameraman, Nihalani is a craftsman. For his first feature film *Aakrosh* (The Cry of the Wounded), he is his own cameraman, and a director, and the fusion gives us much insight into the man.

I use the term craftsman advisedly, because Nihalani's technical background sets him apart from his contemporaries who are bracketed into the terminology of the New Cinema Movement in India at present.

For ten years, he worked through an apprenticeship within the framework of the film industry in Bombay, as assistant to cinematographer V. K. Murthy. Theoretical differentiation between the industry and his own reference points is not something he dwells upon. They have, however, sharpened his awareness of the technical and financial resources available to a low budget film maker. The transition from cameraman to director seems the smoother for his active involvement and understanding of the changing shape of the film industry in these areas. He can offer constructive and reasoned arguments on the part government finance can play in promoting low budget films; he could also maximise his own resources by shooting *Aakrosh* entirely in 16 mm colour, push it to a 35 mm blow-up print, and justifiably be satisfied with the result. (16 mm processing, and its use for feature films is very much in a trial stage in India, and facilities for mixing are cumbersome and limited). At the same time, he is aware of the grammar and skills of an Indian film tradition which stretches back decades.

His association with Shyam Benegal as cameraman on all his feature films was perhaps a catalyst period. Benegal's films showed that "art" and commercial cinema are not necessarily antithetical terms or divorced from a continuous process of development, that the medium was acceptable, viable and could project powerful statements that could sharpen audience awareness. To some of the New Cinema film makers, the film as an opposition force becomes the raison d'etre; the statement itself carries force. To Nihalani, it seems to become a mechanism of growth, both technically and personally.

There is, in Govind, a paradoxical quality of the theatre, as if in some recess of his mind he marshals all he sees and does with the objective of projection. When he talks of friends, they are likely to be drawn from a tight tribe of film or theatre people. To the point where theatrical expression moves into film, or possible films. Many years ago, he co-produced a film with

131

Satyadev Dubey, noted in Hindi and Marathi theatre as a director. It was Vijay Tendulkar's *Shantata Court Chalu Ahe* (Silence! The Court is in Session), dealing, interestingly, like *Aakrosh,* with the victim of a courtroom. It was very much a filmed play, which *Aakrosh* is not, though at times one may find in it elements of theatricality. Dubey is the dialogue writer for many of Benegal's films. Tendulkar is the scenarist of *Aakrosh.* Lines within lines, and a continuing connection, over many years.

There is another aspect of Govind's work, one that could be ignored quite easily in assessing him, if one did not realise that a discipline was being evolved which is reflected quite unconsciously in his film *Aakrosh.*

I come back, inexorably, to Nihalani, the technician.

For as long as he worked with features, he was also a leading documentary and advertising film cameraman. I believe that it is in this period, which covers almost twelve years of his professional life, that the craftsman in Govind experimented and honed his technical work. What was required was the ability to encapsulate information, to sift out the importance of the instant event. The late documentary film maker, S. Sukhdev, also a director-cameraman, who influenced many of us in the late sixties and early seventies, had the same innate sense of visual precision, of involving us in a rich collage of personal vision. But he was not successful in transferring it to feature films. Nihalani ranges between the documentarist's observation and a sense of theatrical presentation, a film technician making fiction out of reality, with much more assurance.

Almost twelve years separate my first encounter with Govind, and the latest. In 1969, he was cameraman on my documentary, *Ashiana* (The Nest). In 1980, he was director-cameraman, Second Unit, of Richard Attenborough's *Gandhi,* on which I also worked.

There could hardly be a greater contrast in scale, or of the experience and professional ability Nihalani had developed in the years between.

For *Ashiana,* he had to work in the rough with a small wind-up 16 mm Bolex using time-expired stock. For *Gandhi,* he had the command of Panavision and a mini-army of supports, working on the largest film production undertaken in India. Different, but the same. In Amritsar, near the Golden Temple for General Dyer's move towards the massacre at Jalianwallabagh, the light was fading, the crowds confining. Nihalani impetuously lifted the heavy Panavision camera and waded in for his shots. "Documentary training," he said laconically.

The point becomes elliptical. Richard Attenborough chose him for the Gandhi film because he saw *Aakrosh.* And it is entirely fitting that in the middle of Nihalani's work on *Gandhi* he won the Golden Peacock Award at the 8th International Film Festival of India for *Aakrosh.*

Shama Habibullah

AAKROSH
(Cry of the Wounded)

1980/Col/144 mins/Hindi
Direction/Camera
Govind Nihalani
Produced by
Devi Dutt, Narayan Kenny
Story/Screenplay
Vijay Tendulkar
Music
Ajit Varman
Editing
Keshav Naidu
Art
C. S. Bhatti
Lead Players
Naseeruddin Shah
(Bhaskar Kulkarni),
Smita Patil (Nagi),
Amrish Puri (Dussane),
Om Puri (Lahanya Bhiku),
Arvind Deshpande (Dr. Patil),
Dr. Mohan Agashe
(Town Council President),
Achut Potdar
(Forest Contractor),
Nana Palsikar
(Lahanya's father),
Bhagyasree Kotnis
(Sheeta, Lahanya's sister),
Mahesh Elkunchwar
(Social worker)
Enquiries
Krsna Movies Enterprises,
9 Little Gift, 19th Rd.,
Khar, Bombay 400 052.
Tel: 538128
OR
National Film Development
Corporation, 13/16 Regent
Chambers, 208 Nariman Point,
Bombay 400 021
Tel: 232218/232183
Grams: Filmvitaran

The tribal's lone cry of rage and anguish.

Memories of his wife haunt Lahanya in his prison cell.

The Adivasis are a tribal community which is denied a caste and therefore very vulnerable. They are referred to as a scheduled tribe. The government is trying to rid them of their stigma by giving them special advantages in education and jobs.

Lahanya Bhiku, an illiterate Adivasi accused of killing his wife, says not a word in protest, either to Bhaskar Kulkarni, the young brahmin lawyer appointed by the court for his defence, or at the trial. This is Kulkarni's first

133

independent, major case, and naturally he is anxious to win it.

Disturbed and exasperated by this obstinate silence Bhaskar Kulkarni investigates on his own. He discovers that Lahanya's wife had been raped and murdered by a combine of local officials, businessmen and politicians. They form the power elite who are beyond the reach of the law. The police are there to support these people, not to protect their victims, for whom the distinctions between State and society have ceased to exist.

True, there are dedicated workers, like the young leftist working among the tribals. He tries at the risk of his life to organize them. But the process of changing attitudes of fear and distrust is long. The problems confronting them are overwhelming and the apparatus used against them unmitigated in its ruthlessness. The local power groups — the contractor, the doctor, the police — can twist the apparatus of the State to their own ends; any one who opposes them is ruthlessly suppressed or bought over even in a court of law.

The terror in this film is a very exact representation of the terror unleashed by vested interests and power groups. The young lawyer, through the same process of being "educated" as the young tribal, learns how helpless he is despite the advantage of an education and a familiarity with the law.

Kulkarni, who takes up Lahanya's case as a professional assignment, gets more involved. Slowly, professional involvement turns into social commitment. This brings him into conflict with his mentor, the public prosecutor, Mr. Dussane, who has chosen to ignore what happens outside the four walls of the courtroom. Ironically he too comes of tribal stock, but has had the benefit of education and is rewarded with a job. Mr Dussane is not unaware of the truth but he has chosen to come to terms with the system: he is himself kept in line by a stream of invective and threats over late-night telephone calls.

The decadence of the vested interests is underlined by the sequence of the *tamasha* and dancing girl. The *tamasha* in Maharashtra is populist "commedia," often with biting social satire. Here, it has been used to mirror the vulgarity of the power group.

In this surround, lip service is paid to tradition, in the sense that the tribal can be released from prison to perform his father's funeral rites which only a son can do. But he remains literally and figuratively in shackles. For him, liberation can only mean death. It is a decision that may lead Bhaskar Kulkarni to the same conclusion.

Lahanya's silence forces the viewer to ask why this is so, why he never makes an attempt to say anything. We begin by being impatient with what appears to be his stupidity and his stubbornness. We gradually learn a lesson he himself has had to learn. If he speaks nobody will believe him. Life will become even more dangerous for those he has left behind: his aged father and his young sister.

Nihalani also keeps the lensing and visuals emphatic with only rare indulgent visual effects at times that do not detract from the pungency, moral fervour and overall effectiveness of this fine first film.

Gene Moskowitz
Variety (U.S.A)
January 28, 1980

Aakrosh is a searing indictment of this system and the society which it sustains. The indictment is made without rhetoric, without sloganeering, without table-thumping propaganda. It is made quietly, lucidly, systematically and, mostly, non-ideologically.

Anil Dharkar
Debonair fortnightly magazine

Filmography

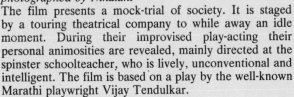

1971 **SHANTATA COURT CHALU AHE**
(Silence! The Court is in Session)
B&W/120 mins/Marathi
Co-production with Satyadev Dubey (Director) and photographed by Nihalani
The film presents a mock-trial of society. It is staged by a touring theatrical company to while away an idle moment. During their improvised play-acting their personal animosities are revealed, mainly directed at the spinster schoolteacher, who is lively, unconventional and intelligent. The film is based on a play by the well-known Marathi playwright Vijay Tendulkar.

1979 **A FINE TOLERANCE** (documentary)
Col/20 mins
A promotional film made for Cooper Engineering Works, part of the Walchand Group of industries. It was meant for the Hamburg International Engineering Fair to present their range of machine tools.

WOMB OF POWER (documentary)
Col/20 mins
Made for Walchand Nagar Industries, a part of the Walchand Group, to present the corporate image and highlight the nuclear jobs made for various nuclear power reactors in the country.

Nihalani has the following three films in mind as a director. One is based on a Hindi novel by Bhishm Sahni set against the background of the partition of India. It is the story of suffering and anguish of an entire population caught in the division of the country.
The second is on a script by Mahesh Elkunchwar, a Marathi playwright. It is based on his play 'Party' and is a scathing comment on middle class hypocrisies. The third is *Surya* (The Sun) a story by S.D. Panwalkar and scripted by Vijay Tendulkar. Ostensibly an exploration of the relationship between a father and son against the background of the police force, the film attempts to relate the deep-rooted corruption and decay in the law-keeping force to the decadence and degeneration of values in society as a whole. The film is set in contemporary Bombay.

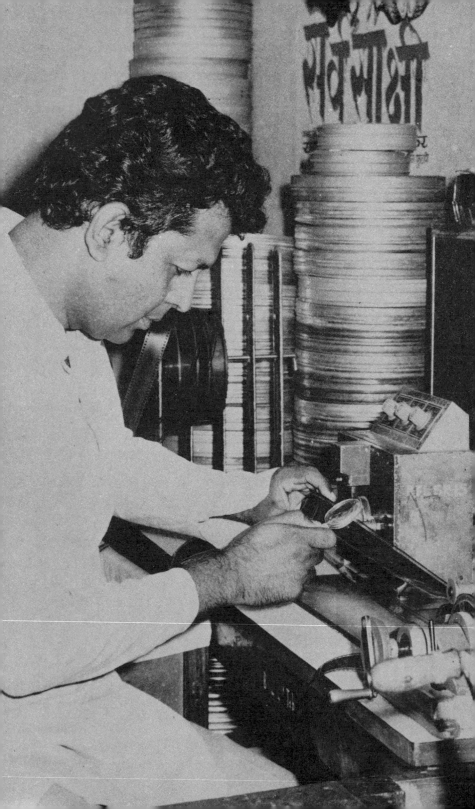

RAMDAS PHUTANE

Ramdas Phutane attempts
to fight in *Sarvasakshi*
against the weight of
traditions which impose a
type of feudal relationship
in the villages, still
nowadays, and he also
opposes forced marriages.
His hyper-realistic
description of the social
context adds to the cruelty
of the events.

Jean-Pierre Brossard
(*'Impartial*
In a series titled
'The thousand faces
of Indian cinema'.)
March 22/23, 1980

Ramdas started his career on a conventional note: as an art teacher in the Marwari Mahavidyalaya of Bombay where he spent 12 years. At the same time he wrote articles for the Hindi tabloids and edited a Hindi annual of his own. He even published a collection of poems — 'Cut-piece and Other Poems'.

I have known him since these early days when he used to bring his annual publication for review to the papers. Nobody would have imagined that very soon he would enter the Marathi film industry with a bang.

Ramdas is from a traditional 30-member joint family, still living together in the district town of Jamkhed. He acknowledges that it is an economically backward place, where social mores have remained unchanged, and to which he is intensely loyal. No one else in the family, including his wife, is interested in films. They feel the money could have fetched better returns if it were invested in the family business, cloth and garments.

For *Saamna* (Confrontation), the first film he produced, Ramdas got together a highly talented team. Vijay Tendulkar, eminent Marathi playwright just venturing into script-writing, wrote an original screenplay for the film. For Jabbar Patel, it meant his first film as a director: he had directed the sensational stage success 'Ghashiram Kotwal' written by Tendulkar.

"When I saw 'Ghashiram' 'Phutane told me,' I felt I could easily entrust Jabbar with a film." Jabbar was hesitant because he did not even know how to hold a camera. Phutane persuaded Jabbar with the confident forecast that he would learn the ropes in 15 days. Phutane admits that a certain staginess was inevitable in the film because the unit was drawn from the theatre.

"With our very first film, we selected a theme which was at the heart of politics in Maharashtra," explained the producer. "We hit hard at the political bosses in the districts, who are effective king-makers."

The portrayal of the small-time political tyrant went home so well that there were attempts by the real-life prototypes of this character to have the film banned. The press picked up the scent of potential political muzzling of the film and publicised it. The film had a halting run but won a National Award.

Fortunately, it was entered at the Berlin Film Festival. Phutane visited Berlin with leading members of his cast and director Jabbar Patel. I remember him visiting me on the eve of his departure and insisting I write short bio-datas of the artists concerned. I was ill at the time and could barely oblige him. Then, in an unexpectedly touching gesture, he thrust fifty rupees ($7) in my hand and stalked away. This traditional gesture has complex associations. It is a propitiatory offering to Laxmi, the goddess of prosperity. Such an offer cannot

137

A memorable shot towards the end: when the teacher is freed and the *bhagat* jailed, their eyes meet, no word is exchanged, and one is startled at the thought that the witch doctor and the modern man are perhaps two halves of the same creature.

Elliott Stein
Film Comment (U.S.A.)
May/June 1980

be refused. It was as if he considered my writing some what auspicious for the success of his film. It was senti mental behaviour quite in tune with his flamboyance

It is precisely this attitude which binds his actor. and technicians to him even when he is in straits and has to re-arrange urgent payments like a pack of cards Perhaps, the young school teacher who is the hero of hi own directorial venture, *Sarvasakshi* The Omniscient), is reflection of his own self: youthful, earnest and emotiona

The Berlin trip changed Phutane's fortunes com pletely. With its subsequent publicity, *Saamna* enjoyee a galloping run on re-issue. At this very time, the Government of Maharashtra introduced a scheme for sizeable refund of the entertainment tax collected on Marathi films. Provided the producer started on a second venture, this part of the tax was made over to him.

With the same sanguine confidence he displayed as a producer, Ramdas directed his first feature, *Sarvasakshi.* The original story was based on superstitious murders tha rocked Maharashtra. He shot the film in his native Jamkhed

During the shooting, another son of the village Dr. Arole, and his wife, received the Magsaysay Awarc of the Philippines for their work in the field of Rura Health. Ramdas quickly organised a reception for the couple, a gesture quite in the spirit of the film, which shows the school teacher trying to introduce a number of reforms among the credulous villagers.

Ever since his return from Berlin some years ago Ramdas Phutane has been in the vanguard of the Marathi film makers' movement. He is currently an office bearer of the film industry's apex organisation. He moves swiftly from Bombay to Pune and from Pune to Kolhapur for meetings and participates in delegations calling on ministers.

It is a comic paradox that he should be busy playing a typical State Minister in Bhaskar Chandavarkar's *Attyachar* (Persecution), a Marathi film being produced by the National Film Development Corporation. "I don't ac in my own films. They have to run," he slyly adds.

His forthcoming film, *Jallosh* (Down with Festivals) introduces the work of Ashok Patole, a new young writer. Ramdas attends all the plays in Bombay looking for new actors to play the lead roles. In all his films Ramdas introduces new talent, either actors or technicians

The inherent business acumen is evident as Ramdas reels off the break-up of returns on films, succinctly giving the percentage that goes to the distributor and the theatre owner and the meagre 5% that a producer may sometimes get back.

He has no illusions about the viability of off-beat films against the overpowering onslaught of the big budget commercial films: "It will only do the rounds of the festival circuit and be exhibited by the government.' The buoyant optimism that has sustained him till now will perhaps overcome this passing despondency.

Dnyaneshwar Nadkarni

SARVASAKSHI
(The Omniscient)

The bhagat's *power of propitiation drawing on blind superstition.*

B&W/135 mins/1979/Marathi
Direction, Produced by & Story
Ramdas Phutane
Camera
Sharad Navle
Editing
N.S. Vaidya
Music
Bhaskar Chandavarkar
Art Direction
Dinanath Chawhan
Sound
Madhav Patade
Players
Smita Patil (Sujatha),
Jayram Hardikar (Ravi),
Anjali Paigankar (Rekha),
Vijay Joshi (the "bhagat")
Enquiries
Giriraj Pictures, Tulsi Nivas,
61 D Road, Veer Nariman
Road, Bombay 400 020.
Tel: 293697

Ravi, an idealistic school teacher, and his wife Rekha, arrive in the village of Ranjanwadi where the young man joins the staff of a school. Ravi is interested in social work, with a special concern for his pupils. He finds that he has to face a wall of blind tradition and docile belief in practices passed on from generation to generation.

The only people sympathetic to Ravi's efforts are Jadhavrao, a member of the landed gentry, his widowed daughter-in-law Sujata and young grandson Shekhar. The film takes a dramatic turn when it starts portraying the machinations of the *bhagat* who is both a *swami* and a witch doctor. Rekha is now pregnant. She has a strong premonition that at child-birth either she or her child will die. She goes to the *bhagat* in the hope that such an outcome will be averted with his blessings. He demands a human sacrifice which the horrified Rekha refuses to consider. Rekha dies while giving birth and Ravi's rationalism is obscured with doubt.

Ravi too is unwittingly embroiled in the *bhagat's* power-play when he is charged with the murder of one of the *bhagat's* victims. In his prison cell, his vision of a young boy being sacrificed on a nearby hill is confirmed. The police acting on his premonition catch the *bhagat* and the school head-master in ritualistic preparation for

Ramdas Phutane looks like the typical Maratha (the martial race of Maharashtra), tall swarthy and well built. Even upon short acquaintance, one is conscious of a peasant-like tenacity and pride in his roots. He does not want to live in the big cities to be swamped by "the uniform five-star culture of the elite." Time strengthens the impression of a pragmatic outlook leavened with a sense of humour.

the sacrifice. Released from prison, the troubled Ravi wonders if his vision was more than a coincidence.

The film is based on the real-life context of the Manvat murders in Maharashtra. It has been shot entirely on location. The cast, apart from Anjali Paigankar and Smita Patil, has been drawn from the avant garde Marathi stage.

Dnyaneshwar Nadkarn

The bhagat's hypnotic stare that induces suggestion.

Filmography

1976 SAAMNA (Confrontation) (as producer)
B & W/140 mins/Marathi
Lead players: Shreeram Lagoo, Nilu Phule and
Mohan Agashe

The film exposes the corrupt power structure of rural cooperatives. At the apex is the ruthless sugar baron with whom the idealistic and intellectual freedom fighter comes into conflict.

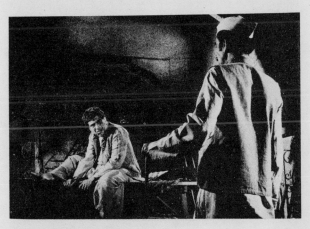

1980 SARVASAKSHI (The Omniscient)
(as director/producer)

1981 Currently working on **Jallosh** (Down With Festivals) which expresses Phutane's concern with outmoded celebrations of festivals. The degeneration is visible in the extortionate money demands and cheap entertainment.

PATTABHI RAMA REDDY

On himself...

"Just before the time my book of poems was written, I had
had a surfeit of the lyrical poetry of Rabindranath Tagore
in the romantic atmosphere of Santiniketan (a university
centre in Bengal) for nearly two years. I joined Calcutta
University for my Master's degree in English Literature
and took up residence in a dingy room on Lower Chitpur
Road in Calcutta. The din, the squalor and the human
misery shocked me to the core. The mad commercial
activity of the city and innocence exploited by avarice,
disturbed me greatly. The gathering war clouds in Europe
completely shattered the misty moonlight influence
of Tagore. It was the year 1938.

All the thousand metaphors I had read in the *Bhava
Kavitvam* (romantic poetry), in *Prabandhams* (classical
epics), and in Tagore's songs, suddenly lost all their meaning.
It was at that moment I found the point of view, rather
the angle of attack which later formed the basis of my
verses. I distinctly felt sick inside me. My heart was
indeed an *asantiniketan* (abode of discontent).

I could no longer continue my studies at Calcutta.
I returned to Nellore, my home in Andhra Pradesh.

I reluctantly entered my family business of Mica export
at Gudur. I used to travel often between Madras and Nellore.
Business life least interested me, though the prospect of
going to the U.S.A. tempted me to stick to it. (In 1940
Pattabhi Rama Reddy went to Columbia University to
study Mathematics, returning to India in 1943 owing to the
outbreak of the World War. *Ed.*)

I used to meet Sri Sri and Mallavarapu Visweswara Rao
(two revolutionary poets) whenever I went to Madras.
It is at this time that I wrote 'Ragala Dozen' (A Dozen
Melodies). With the basic experience of Calcutta providing
my viewpoint, I indented on my observations in Madras
and Nellore to cull the material necessary for my first
book of poems.

The authors who influenced me most were Sri Sri
and Chalam. I read and re-read the prose poems of
Walt Whitman. Oscar Wilde's 'Ballad of Reading Jail'
haunted me constantly. The writing of Freud interested
me a great deal. Above all, the negative influence of
Tagore had a great deal to do with the pattern I en-
visaged for my book. I consciously tried to break away
from his imagery. Another person who made a powerful
impression on me was Albert Einstein, both as a
man and a mathematician. I was amazed by his daringly
original thinking.

Earlier, while in Santiniketan, I experimented a great
deal with end rhymes. I was in search of a new sound.
Tagore had discarded the Sanskrit metres with end rhymes

in Bengali. But this was a singularly difficult task in Telugu because most of the words end in du, mu, vu, lu. Practically every word rhymed with the other. The experiments I made did bear fruit; a considerable body of end rhyme poetry has now come to pass. Of course the end rhymes were not meant to be an end in themselves. It was more a way of trying to change the content as well as style.

But for the agitated feelings I wished to convey I felt I had to find new weapons. I wanted the readers of these poems to sit up and take note. I was even prepared for abuse. It is apathy that kills. Only out of friction can progress be achieved. This also explains why I wrote all the poems in first person singular. Buffoonery, egoism and sex were all part of my arsenal.

I had to find a rhythm that reflected the beat of the city with its cacophony of street noises mingled with human anguish. This ruled out the traditional prose with its incantatory effect. Verse, however revolutionary, lulls one to a sense of well being and satisfaction.

The chaos of the external world could not brook proper grammar. Debunking of established values was essential before a new order could be built. I wanted to peer behind the smug mask that society wears. All these thoughts, though not as explicitly as I mention, were within me when I composed these poems.

Extracts, introduction to **Ragala Dozen** (A Dozen Melodies), published by the Progressive Union, Town Hall, Trunk Road, Nellore, Andhra Pradesh.

Samskara. . .from story to film

Dr. U. R. Ananthamurthy is a leading Kannada short-story writer and novelist whose works have inspired most of Karnataka's younger film makers. As a close friend of the Reddy family, he writes about *Samskara*, (Funeral Rites) one of his earlier stories, and how it almost accidentally and through inspired cooperation, came to be filmed.

The year was 1965. While in Oxford, my tutor Malcolm Bradbury suggested I should write on my experience of centuries co-existing in India. That started me on writing 'Samskara' in Kannada. For me it was an act of self-discovery.

Meanwhile, in India, Girish Karnad had read the manuscript. He and Pattabhi Rama Reddy, along with a visiting Australian cameraman Tom Cowan, had prepared a shot-by-shot film script of it. I returned to India to find Karnad and others with shaven heads and tufts, ready to shoot and act in this film, using a village from my district as its location.

Pattabhi, I know, will permit me to explain what my differences are with the film, as a novelist.

In my novel, the dead man's corpse, halfway through the story, is removed secretly by a Muslim friend of the dead man. Hence the dilemma concerning the cremation by Praneshacharya, the protagonist, becomes a purely metaphysical one. The corpse is symbolic. The last rites of a dead man in the brahmin custom involves not only the burning of the corpse, but makes the dead *Preta* (the unsubstantial body) into a *Pitru* (the ancestor to be worshipped). Does the dead rebel deserve such veneration is the focus of the novel. But Praneshacharya, when he realises all he has in common with his rival after having made love to the dead man's mistress, becomes *the other man* himself, thus embodying the presence of the other within himself. The scriptwriter and the director felt that the body should be kept for the protagonist to return to after his wanderings, cremating it himself as an act of expiation.

Film is not my medium and perhaps Pattabhi and Girish are justified in the changes they made. Yet, I insist that my novel says something different, something more abstract. According to me the corpse is not there *objectively,* but is there for Praneshacharya *subjectively.*

Thus Snehalata and Pattabhi Rama Reddy made my novel their own, and because they made it, sharing as they did a common heritage with me, in our radical anti-caste political tradition, the film was not only an artistic venture but a committed political act. The two were never separate in our minds.

Pattabhi. . . at home

In the midst of the supreme chaos of his chosen existence, Pattabhi Rama Reddy remains unbelievably serene, exuding a saintly benevolence and heroic tolerance. The Reddys run an open house in the quaint family cottage where they live in the heart of Bangalore city. In fact, the front door is never bolted.

People of all kinds, types and ages wander in and out and are miraculously fed and attended to. They range from poets, painters, newspapermen, politicians, worthy elders to nobodies; or wild-haired teenaged or aging musicians or admirers adhering to his son Konarak and his rock group. Konarak is a gifted composer and guitarist.

Social workers, union groups, student leaders, any and everyone in need of help, drop by to visit his lovely, vivacious daughter, Nandana. She conducts a rural education and guidance program and is consultant to various worker's groups. The presence of his wife Snehalata, who died tragically young a few years ago, pervades the house. It is she who gave this home its sunlit warmth, its even-tempered hospitality and its inspired gregarious ambience. Her main trait was that of a true humanist. Her main interest was the theatre.

Pattabhi absorbs the discord and unity that co-exist around him, his own inner aspirations lying dormant. Occasionally, he rouses himself to surface again. . . towards making another film.

Reddy's *Samskara* was a landmark not only in Indian cinema but for all those who pitched into the making of it. Almost every name on its titles is today a leading film and theatre personality who had no idea at that time that *Samskara* was in some way or other to change his or her life.

SAMSKARA
(Funeral Rites)

A tradition-bound community plagued by an undefinable corpse.

1970/B&W/100 mins/
Kannada
Direction/Produced by
Pattabhi Rama Reddy
Story
U. R. Ananthamurthy
Screenplay/Dialogue
Girish Karnad
Camera
Tom Cowan
Music
Rajeev Taranath
Art Direction
S. G. Vasudev
Editing
Steven Cartaw, Vasu
Players
Girish Karnad
(Praneshacharya),
Snehalata Reddy (Chandri),
P. Lankesh (Naranappa),
Dasharathi Dikshit
(Laxmana), Lakshmi
Krishnamurthy (the mad
woman)
Enquiries
Pattabhi Rama Reddy,
58 St. Marks Road,
Bangalore 560 001.
Tel: 52423

Hinduism decrees a specific ritual for every aspect of life. Brahmins as the heirs and custodians of the Scriptures are strictly enjoined to perform all the codified rites.

Samskara portrays the customs of *Madhvas,* a sub-sect of brahmins in South India. They are the devotees of Vishnu, a deity of the Hindu Trinity. The *Madhvas* wear a vertical caste-mark on their forehead. They live in a closeknit village community. The *Smarthas* are another brahmin sub-sect of South India. They are distinguished by three horizontal lines drawn across the forehead. They worship Shiva, another god of the Trinity. A subtle rivalry exists between the two sects.

When a brahmin dies, he has to be cremated with due sacraments to attain salvation. His family and other brahmins may not eat or even drink water until the body is cremated. During the 13-day period of pollution due to death, they may not participate in any religious ritual. Their presence would defile the entire ritual. Even in his everyday life, a brahmin is constantly haunted by the fear of ritual pollution. He can be polluted through food, touch or any close physical contact with a lower caste.

To this community, ridden with a pollution complex, the death of Naranappa, a renegade brahmin, poses an insuperable problem. Naranappa rejoiced in his flamboyant defiance of every caste taboo, including eating meat, drinking liquor and flaunting a loyal low caste mistress, Chandri, before his horrified fellow brahmins. He openly mocked their sanctimonious ways.

Praneshacharya, the protagonist of the film, is a learned and pious man, consulted by the community on spiritual matters. He lives an ascetic life, tending his ailing wife. He is asked to solve the dilemma—whether Naranappa is to be cremated and if so, by whom? In other words, can

The troubled brahmin scholar

Naranappa be considered a brahmin? He ought to have been excommunicated while alive.

Gunda and Laxmana, the two male brahmins related to him, are duty bound to perform the cremation. But both had quarrelled with Naranappa. Chandri gives her jewellery to Praneshacharya to defray the expenses of the cremation. Both Gunda and Laxmana are now lured by the gold and eager to perform their duty.

Acharya spends a fruitless night pouring over the Scriptures to find a solution. Instead, while dreaming, he re-lives his confrontation with a sneering Naranappa. He prays to Lord Maruti, the local deity, for guidance, without any result. He comes upon a patiently waiting Chandri at the temple. He succumbs to sex, not only for long suppressed sexual gratification but for the comfort of her earthy motherliness.

A group of drunken young men initiated by Naranappa to the delights of drink and the glamour of the stage resolve to perform the cremation but are frightened away by the rats swarming everywhere. No one is aware that the rats are the carriers of plague. Prolonged starvation drives one of them (an old man) to sneak in a meal without the others knowing.

The troubled Praneshacharya sends the men from the village to the spiritual guru of the community for his ruling. The women and children leave the village to stay with relatives. Acharya's wife dies the same night.

Acharya sets out on an aimless journey, a metaphorical pilgrimage where he is forced to befriend a gregarious stranger, Putta. He visits the annual festival at the temple, eats with all the other brahmins and runs away when he is recognized. Now he has realised the hypocritical life he had lived. He confesses to Putta and goes back to the village which has been evacuated because of the plague. He will perform the cremation to expiate for his earlier inhuman dogmatism.

Filmography

1977   **CHANDAMARUTHA (Wild Wind)** in which Pattabhi Rama Reddy's late wife Snehalata starred and his daughter Nandana plays an important role. The film is about inner forces, working on a personal as well as social level, rebelling against authoritarianism.

PAPER BOATS (Tentative title) to be made in Kannada and Hindi versions, is based on Pattabhi's own script and story. The film is entirely set around one couple (played by Amol Palekar and Deepa Dhanraj) and deals in a surrealistic way with their romantic and sexual involvement.

Reddy is currently working on a film, scripted by Dr. U. R. Ananthamurthy, about Gandhi and his message. He stresses that there will be no spectacle in this low budget project. It will "unequivocally put forth Gandhi's ideals."

147

M. S. SATHYU

Sathyu reveals an acute
eye for the specific realities
of the Indian experience,
simply and directly
registered.

Verina Glaessner,
**Monthly Film Bulletin
(U.K.)
July 1977**

He smiles easily. A strange child-like quality, totally without guile; a sort of melancholic charm. The eyes remain distant, not sharing the joke, slightly unfocused, a little sad and tired. Streaks of grey in the beard speak of a little suffering. And a face so ravaged by time as to be almost beautiful. The face of an artist. Or a philosopher.

A strange, enigmatic figure. Mystifying. A contradiction. Intensely shy, yet extremely controversial. A very private person, espousing the most public of causes. Given to politicising, but staying clear of politics. He arouses the most fierce loyalty among a certain group of actors and technicians who find him totally committed, intensely driven, utterly brilliant. And there are his detractors, who swear that they would never like to work for him again, accusing him of being totally disorganised, unprofessional and pedestrian.

With his very first film *Garm Hava* (Hot Winds) made in late 1973, Sathyu set off a storm of controversy to the delight of film-buffs, critics, intellectuals and dismayed stodgy bureaucrats. The film was promptly branded pro-Muslim. A fanatic fringe wanted to see Sathyu behind bars. *Garm Hava* was about the anti-Muslim hysteria which swept the country in the months following the partition of the country into India and Pakistan.

Anticipating communal riots, producers withheld the film's release until after the elections. Despite the financial strain caused by the delay, Sathyu was unperturbed. It was his intenstion to expose the bogey, all the sham of secularism.

"What I really wanted to expose in *Garm Hava* was the games these politicians play. Actually there are no human considerations at all. I am not talking only about India, but even in Vietnam, Biafra, Germany . . . it is all the same. How many of us in India really wanted the Partition? Look at all the suffering it caused."

Undue fears are usually belied. *Garm Hava* did not unleash violence or resentment. On the contrary, it left audiences more chastened, sympathetic to communal susceptibilities. The film was a competitive entry in the Cannes Film Festival in 1974, the first Indian film to feature there after a gap of ten years. Its ultimate triumph: the film won India's top award for serving the cause of "National Integration."

Despite all the critical raves, financially the film turned out to be a squib. There were huge debts and Sathyu had no idea how he was going to meet them. There was a lot of harrassment from financial institutions.

"It was a nightmare. Sometimes I think I would have been better off not making *Garm Hava.* There were offers to make the usual commercial formula kind of stuff. It was very tempting and I was desperate, but I just kept refusing. I don't think it is very easy to make that kind of

149

successful trash. You've got to be genuinely vulgar to make vulgar films."

Two years of inactivity followed. Then came *Kanneshwara Rama* (The Legendary Outlaw) inspired by a folklore character from the South, a kind of a latter-day Robin Hood. The film fared well financially, but it had a sterile, plastic quality, and from an artistic point of view did little credit to Sathyu.

"It was not a question of letting people down," Sathyu admitted. "I let myself down."

Sathyu's own life could well be the story of a film. A father wanting his son to be a scientist or an engineer. The son had grand designs of becoming a film maker. The small-town chap (from Mysore) arrives in the big bad city (Bombay), armed with a little talent and a soaring ambition to take over the film world. Within a few days of his arrival the rosy dreams are shattered.

Sathyu muses about those days. "I couldn't get a job. I was a very timid fellow, and could not even get beyond the Nepalese watchman guarding the studio entrance." He could not afford to lose face, so he wrote to his father and pretended to be doing very well, and asked him to discontinue the Rs. 50 (approximately eight dollars) monthly allowance. "In those days I could not afford to travel by bus. I sold the newspaper, 'Bombay Youth', for 10 paise each outside Churchgate station."

He was always interested in theatre and took to set-designing. His first assignment was for the English-elite Theatre Group production of 'Othello'. To make ends meet he took to art direction in films, winning an award for the art direction of *Haqeeqat* (The Fact) in 1965.

Theatre, however, remained a passion. Sathyu joined IPTA (Indian People's Theatre Association), a Hindustani theatre group with leftist leanings. From stage designing he went to direction. His choice of plays showed a very eclectic mind. A historical ('Mirza Ghalib'), a musical ('Mitti Ki Gadi'—The Clay Cart), a political satire ('Bakri'—Sheep), and the recent 'Sufaid Kundali,' an adaptation of 'The Caucasian Chalk Circle'.

Although Sathyu has achieved considerable success in theatre, his forte will always be cinema. The kind of brilliance that was evident in *Garm Hava* indicated a superb cinematic vision, and a sure confidence in handling the narrative form. Sathyu is now in the process of shooting his new film *Kahan Kahan se Guzar Gaya* (The Search), a film about today's youth. He feels they are hopelessly confused and are being misled by vested interests: "The education in this country doesn't lead to anything at all. Something is wrong with the basic system. I do not think Satyajit Ray said it emphatically enough in *Pratidwandi* (The Adversary)."

With a wistful smile Sathyu talks about his future projects. "I want to make all sorts of films and not be branded. A love story to fulfil the softer side of my nature. I've got ideas for an out-and-out comedy, for a ballet film, a children's film . . . . I'm very ambitious that way." To prove it, each of his films has had a totally different theme and style. For a moment his eyes light up, and he appears soft and vulnerable. There's all the excitement of a child of the cinema.

Arun Sachdev

Sathyu's diverse and catholic tastes are evident in his interests and his personal life. He is at home in South India (where he was born in an orthodox brahmin family), Bombay (where he lives) and Delhi (where he worked in theatre). He knows the languages of these areas. He stages plays mostly in Hindi, Urdu and Kannada. His wife, Shama Zaidi, is a Muslim. She is a leading scriptwriter and works closely with her husband on his films. Sathyu is also a considerate parent and he dotes on his two daughters. . . an affable family man at home, and a vocal, aggressive rebel outside of it.

I am not denying that the Hindus too have suffered under the Muslim rule. It is an age-old wound that has been carried on and on, but nobody wants to talk about it. You want to hush it up, to pretend it doesn't exist. Unless you discuss it openly and try to understand the problem, you are not going to solve it by just hiding it.

M.S. Sathyu

GARM HAVA
(Hot Winds)

Amina, happy and in love, shares her joy with an understanding grandmother.

1975 Col/136 mins/Urdu
Direction
M. S. Sathyu
Produced by
*M. S. Sathyu, Abu Siwani
and Ishan Arya*
Story
*Kaifi Azmi
(based on an unpublished
short story by Ismat Chugtai)*
Screenplay
Kaifi Azmi, Shama Zaidi
Camera
Ishan Arya
Music
Ustad Bahadur Khan
Editing
S. Chakraborty
Players
*Balraj Sahni (Salim Mirza),
Dinanath Zutshi (Halim Mirza)
Badar Begum ("Dadi Amma"
Salim Mirza's mother),
Gita (Amina), Abu Siwani
(Baqar Mirza),
Farouque Shaikh
(Sikandar), Jamal Hashmi
(Kazim), Yunus Parwaiz
(Fakhruddin), Jalal Agha
(Shamshad).*

Garm Hava means the "burning wind," the wind that scorched the two countries, India and Pakistan, carved out of the Indian subcontinent in 1947.

The film, within the microcosm of a Muslim family in Agra, gives a human dimension to our understanding of the larger event. It also has universal implications in its reflection of the personal tragedies of lands and families, to the questioning of loyalties, to the inflaming of deep-rooted prejudices and, above all, the tearing out of wide-spreading, centuries-old roots. On both sides of the border, millions were made into refugees. It is remarkable that the film *Garm Hava* can deal with the context of violence by showing none, that the delicacy of treatment can draw out the personal anguish of a community with such authority and strength.

Salim Mirza is a middle-aged Muslim trader whose family have for generations been shoe manufacturers in Northern India. Their family, like most Muslim ones thereafter, reflects the conflicts of Partition. To some, the move was to the Promised Land; to others, to a possible El Dorado. But a heart-breakingly large number fled for their lives from the violent upheavals that bloodied the birth of the two countries.

Salim Mirza's conniving elder brother Halim emigrates after much show of national leadership to the new country of Pakistan with his wife and son Kazim. But Salim

A disillusioned Amina

Mirza sees no reason to change his homeland for another. His roots are deep. A man of principle and integrity, he is respected by his neighbours. He stays on to look after the family business and his home.

Halim's son Kazim, in love with and engaged to Salim's daughter Amina, is unable to return to India because larger political events have sealed the border. No one had visualised that violence and war would cut off hitherto united families so completely from one another. Kazim eventually manages to slip across the border to see Amina in order to marry her, even though a marriage has been arranged for him in Pakistan. In the midst of the hurried preparations for a wedding, the police arrest Kazim for illegal entry and take him away. Salim can only watch helplessly Amina's subsequent anguish and withdrawal.

The tentacles of tragedy spread. The ancestral house had been the home of a family living as a customary joint family. But as it is in Halim, the eldest brother's name, it is declared evacuee property. A Sindhi businessman, Ajmani, is allocated the house under a law passed to give refugees coming into the country the property of those who had left.

Salim Mirza is forced to leave his house and find rented accommodation elsewhere. In one of the most moving scenes of the film, the oldest member of the family hides in a dark recess. To her ancient mind the world outside is alien and full of terrors from which the house had sheltered her during a lifetime of traditional seclusion.

Salim's business begins to suffer. No one will advance him money. There is mistrust where there was none; it is felt that Salim might leave the country and not repay the loan, or even that his business might profitably be taken over by others. Refugees from Sind and Punjab have moved into the leather trade. Salim cannot compete with them or with new methods of business. Yet he resists the pressure to leave Agra, to leave all that is known to him. He has faith in his family and the country, divided though it is.

Even this begins to be drawn into question. His younger son has a degree. But there are no jobs, especially for Muslims, the legacy of distrust and turmoil.

Shamshad, another of Amina's cousins, exploits her despondency. It is a seduction with the promise of marriage. Shamshad's self-serving father, who reacts to the changes around him like a weather-vane, flees across the border to avoid debtors. Shamshad goes with him. Finally news comes that he will be married in Pakistan. Amina has been betrayed twice. Once by circumstances, once by Shamshad. Her spirit and her beliefs are shattered. She commits suicide.

Salim Mirza, a broken man, moves towards the step he has resisted for so long. He prepares to leave the country. On the way to the station, he permits his son to join a procession of people protesting against injustice. It symbolises a turning from the past towards the future; a

Remarkably mature both politically and cinematically, this film is directed with rare delicacy. Several scenes — notably the death of the old grand-mother, at last recapturing her lost memories of her wedding day so long ago — are worthy of Satyajit Ray.

Tom Hutchinson
Sunday Telegraph (U.K.)
May 25, 1975

rejection of the forces of despair, destruction and death; and an affirmation of hope. He too joins the procession.

This was an ending requested by Balraj Sahni in this, his last film, which has become a tribute to one of India's great actors. His Salim is restrained, dignified, compassionate and committed.

The tragic content of *Garm Hava* becomes a classic document of human dignity against the inhuman aspects of historical events.

Attia Hosain

Filmography

1969   GHALIB (documentary)
B&W/22 mins
A sensitively made biography of the Urdu poet (1797-1869) whose verses are still loved. The film reflects Ghalib's frustration and repeated attempts to escape from poverty into the freedom of unfettered wandering. The images are drawn from contemporary miniatures, monuments and drawings, and the soundtrack consists entirely of Ghalib's own words, translated into English subtitles.

1977   KANNESHWARA RAMA (The Legendary Outlaw)
Col/137 mins/Kannada and Hindi versions
Lead players: *Anant Nag, Shabana Azmi,*
Amol Palekar, B. V. Karanth
In this second film, Sathyu shifts the scene to the densely forested hills of Malnad in his native Karnataka. It traces retrospectively the tumultuous career of a simple peasant transformed into a Robin Hood-like legendary outlaw, challenging the British in the nascent days of non-violence — the twenties. Rama is finally betrayed by his mistress, the person closest to him. Both of them realise too late the tragedy of betrayal and vindictiveness. The film adopts the folk technique of narrating the story through a ballad at the beginning which serves as an allegorical backdrop.

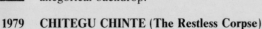

1979   CHITEGU CHINTE (The Restless Corpse)
Col/129 mins/Kannada
Lead players: *C. R. Simha, Ram Prakash, Paula*
Lindsay
Political comment was implicit in Sathyu's earlier films. In this broad-spectrum farcical satire set in an imaginary island (not difficult to identify) Sathyu hits hard at political "bossism," actor-leaders and the formula film. The narrative is complicated but the spoofing is fun.

1980   BARA (The Famine)
Col/140 mins/Kannada and Hindi versions
Lead players: *Anant Nag, Lavleen Madhu*
This film is set in a perenially drought stricken area of Karnataka. It depicts the conflict between bureaucrats

and politicians. Sathyu has tried to expose the interference of politicians even when it concerns the distribution of food to calamity hit areas in spite of the efforts of an idealistic administrator.

1981 **KAHAN KAHAN SE GUZAR GAYA (The Search)**
Col/Hindi
Lead players: Sharon Prabhakar, Anil Kapoor, Nitin Sethi, Neesha Singh, Rita Rani Kaul
This is the latest film under production and produced with the help of the West Bengal Government. Sathyu says, "The film is about the state of helplessness in youth, about their drifting away from responsibilities. I have tried to say that the whole system is to be blamed for this. The degenerate system is producing nothing but mediocrities. There will be no hero in the accepted sense of the term in my film."

Still from Kahan Kahan se Guzar Gaya *(The Search).*

Sathyu has produced over 20 short films and 12 documentaries (one which is highly regarded is on the Urdu poet Ghalib). He also made two films for Children's Film Society, one short on the Indian mime artist, Irshad Panjatan, and the other a feature *Ek tha Chhotu, ek tha Motu* (One was Tiny, the Other, Fat). Sathyu has worked as art director on three films. He is very active in theatre. His current play 'Sufaid Kundali', based on 'The Caucasian Chalk Circle' with Shabana Azmi playing the lead role, has been very successful.

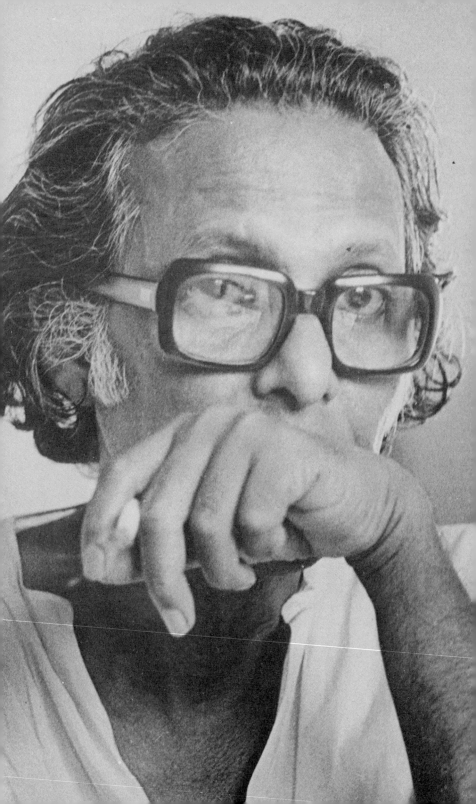

MRINAL SEN

I can't deliberately make a popular film. . . . Indian audiences seek escape from their daily lives when they go to the cinema — my subjects are too close to daily life for popular appeal. I have to find a way to put across my message more successfully. Meanwhile I look for wider audiences overseas.
I feel it is not enough to disturb the audience: it is also necessary to act as an agent provocateur . . . A film must project contemporary attitudes.

Mrinal Sen
**South China
Morning Post
April 16, 1980**

Mrinal was born and brought up in East Bengal (now Bangladesh) and came to Calcutta only in his late teens to study Science. There is no trace of the trauma of Partition, nor any nostalgia for a lost world in his sensibility. This is exceptional in a Bengali of Mrinal's generation — his entire memory seems to be dominated by Calcutta. Particularly in his last two films and the one he is making now, he seems to have evolved almost a formula for his work. He works in concentrated locations (never going beyond a radius of about a dozen miles), finishes shooting in about three weeks, and brings in the completed film in something like six to seven months. He makes his films at a low cost — the budget hardly ever exceeds 70,000 dollars. Low budget is an act of faith for him — he subjects his entire unit and the cast to the discipline of hard work and modest living conditions. A combination of cinematic fluency and austerity of implementation has made Mrinal the exemplar for young cinema in India.

At Berlin while he was receiving the Silver Bear in February for his *Aakaler Sandhaney* (In Search of Famine) he was already committing his next film (at that time just the germ of an idea) for Venice in September, an astonishing display of confidence in a rather difficult environment. The shooting of this film, *Chaalchitra* (Kaleidoscope) is to be over by the middle of May.

Mrinal is now in a happy position where he has no trouble finding financiers or as Mrinal quaintly calls them: "money backers." His film evolves through a series of innovations, locations suggesting business, actors interacting with him to produce dialogue and finally a free-for-all at the cutting stage. This highly innovative film making is not always fruitful. But even when it fails, it affects you with the infectious enthusiasm of the director. It is almost like the delight a child takes in a new toy. Mrinal is so fascinated by the medium, so concerned that the world should know and share his delight, that he sometimes digresses, becomes repetitious, almost strays off from his main theme, until he gets carried away to the extent of making the medium the message. This happened to a number of his films in the past and although this can always happen again, a growing mastery over the medium aided by his indispensible cameraman, Mahajan, now imposes an inbuilt discipline, strengthening rather than diminishing the thematic exposition.

It is, of course, a limited genre, rather like a TV series; each film is an episode on contemporary Bengali middle class life. Yet in two of his rural films, *Matira Manisha* (Two brothers) in Oriya and *Oka Oori Katha* (The Outsiders) in Telugu — both based on classical literature and both languages foreign to Mrinal — he came close to telling epic stories.

**Sen's films are
characteristically mordant,
critical, acutely sensitive
to nuances of social and
human relationships.**

David Robinson
**The Times (U.K.)
January 23, 1976**

While Mrinal is working out his Calcutta cycle, he is already planning to do a film about a peasant and a shepherd. The story is by Premchand, perhaps the greatest writer on the subject of Indian village. I have been close to Mrinal and his work for 25 years—sometimes censorious of his instant cinema, but always impressed by his capacity for renewal and energy—hoping that in the peasant/shepherd project he will not work to a festival deadline but find fulfilment in making a film about the eternal verities.

Years of poverty complicated by the middle class need to keep up appearances provide Mrinal with the hard core inspiraion for his art. The savage selfishness, the cruelty and meanness, the bitterness and crushing hypocrisy of the middle class—it is all there in his work but illuminated by love and compassion. Mrinal has understood the frailty of man. Compassion for the imperfect brings intimations of human nobility in his films. He has earned the right to mock by mocking himself. All the bitterness is eventually washed away by his never-failing sense of humour.

Take an example. Nowhere in the world prevails such fantastic freedom of urination as in Calcutta city. So a man taking a leak against the wall of someone's house is a matter of very little concern. In Mrinal's film (*Ekdin Pratidin* which he has chosen to translate as 'And Quiet Rolls the Dawn' while 'Day In, Day Out' or 'One Day, Every Day' would have been a much more idiomatic translation), however, the irate landlord berates the pisser and the poor fellow mumbles an apologetic "sorry." In a sense the episode is highly unrealistic. Everyone is pissing everywhere in the city—so in the first place, this will hardly cause any comment, let alone admonition. Secondly, the accused party is more likely to feel aggrieved if any one challenges his fundamental right of free urination. In fact the chances are that he will turn very rude and even violent. So Mrinal interjects almost an element of sub-realism with the very Bengali "Sori"— transforms and twists a trivial piece of everyday reality into something quite funny even while he fleshes out the character of the landlord, comments upon the anatomy of the city—Calcutta, his home and obsession, the background for all his urban films.

Mrinal is an imp par excellence. The urge to thumb his nose at authority is an integral part of his character. Mrinal, willy-nilly, is very much a part of the intellectual/ artistic elite of the country but that doesn't stop him from making rude anti-establishment noises. Thus, inspite of receiving the *Padmabhushan* (a high national honour, one of the other recipients this year was Ravi Shankar) and a basket of awards in this year's National Film Festival (Best Film, Best Direction, Best Screenplay—cash awards totalling $7000 tax free—a handsome amount by Indian standards), Mrinal promptly challenged and attacked the conventional assumptions of the venerable Jury Chairman about good cinema.

In a tropical climate, with its inevitable train of diseases and infections, pollution of water and adulteration of food — it is no easy task to remain continuously in good health. It has to be a special genetic gift, a dispensation from the gods. Slight, wiry Mrinal is astonishingly fit at the age of 58. He is never ill, hardly ever tired. The only signs of age are his elegantly greying whiskers.

Mrinal doesn't have a contemplative face. He is never still for a moment. His best portrait would be like one of those Gjon Mili multiple-exposure photographs. He is either talking or gesticulating, generally both. He has a truly astounding capacity for verbalisation — astounding even in terms of a culture that thrives on verbalisation. It is as if words are emerging in a never-ending procession from some dark recess of his unconscious, perhaps even racial memory. Suddenly he grabs hold of an idea even while he utters it, with a reflex alertness akin to that of the dedicated lepidopterist. Some of these butterflies spread their wings in his films. Talking to others, talking to himself — this infinite capacity for conversation gives his films their topical strength, their air of easy uninhibited flow.

We have had many exciting films from Mrinal. It is now time for a masterpiece.

Santi P. Chowdhury

Mrinal Sen, directing on location; towel on shoulder, milkless tea in hand, tireless as ever...

BHUVAN SHOME

The village girl, placing a turban on an embarrassed Bhuvan Shome, the true-blue bureaucrat.

1969/B&W/96 mins/Hindi
Language
Hindi
Direction/Screenplay
Mrinal Sen
Produced by
Mrinal Sen Productions
Camera
K. K. Mahajan
Music
Vijay Raghava Rao
Editing
Gangadhar Naskar
Players
Suhasini Mulay (Gauri),
Utpal Dutt (Bhuvan Shome),
Sadhu Meher (Jadhav Patel),
Shekhar Chatterjee
(Cart Driver)
Enquiries
National Film Development
Corporation,
13/16 Regent Chambers,
Nariman Point,
Bombay 400 021.
Tel: 231861/231832

In post-Independence India (the late forties) Bhuvan Shome, a middle-aged, lonely widower, is a representative of the educated elite raised in the colonial tradition. A relic of Indian Victoriana, he pursues his duties as senior officer of the Indian railways, with such self righteous discipline that when he discovers his son guilty of a minor misdemeanour, he promptly sacks him for "gross" negligence of duty.

But one day, after years of tireless service, he feels terribly bored with his desk-bound routine. He decides to allow himself a short duck-shooting expedition to a remote shore-line of Gujarat, quite fancying himself in the role of an ornithologist. Before leaving, he peremptorily issues orders to sack a young ticket collector, Jadhav Patel, for accepting a bribe.

The carefree new world which Bhuvan Shome slowly walks into, opens a new chapter in his life. He escapes from the confines of his dreary office-walled world to freedom and freshness. It is the world of simple unsophisticated folk living in affinity with nature, speaking a different language, bearing different values. For Bhuvan Shome this outing becomes almost a spiritual journey at the end of which this stern, terrible man is considerably "tamed

160

His bones thoroughly rattled by the long bullock-cart drive, Bhuvan Shome is taught by the weird cart-driver, something of a "linguist," how to bear the hazards of a speeding bullock-cart with fortitude. A marauding buffalo makes him abandon his city-bred inhibitions along with his gear and run for his life and even climb a tree for safety. A man who guides him through the sugarcane fields serves as an example of simple goodness.

And finally Bhuvan Shome meets Gauri, a cheeky young village girl: friendly, casual and graceful, throbbing with vitality. A steady rapport develops between the dissimilar two soon after they meet.

He comes to know that she is the wife of Jadhav Patel. Through various experiences during the day Shome's uncompromising discipline begins to weaken. In the process, Gauri influences Shome's concept of life and people and perhaps also heightens his sense of isolation. On his return from his holiday, Shome surprises everyone by not pressing for Patel's dismissal. He is liberated from his overbearing rectitude, shocking his colleagues by his uncharacteristic, almost boisterous, behavior while at work.

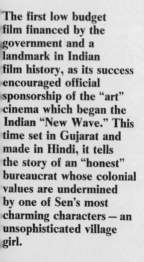

Gauri, the saucy village girl, who brings the city bureaucrat a perception of life's possible eccentricities.

The first low budget film financed by the government and a landmark in Indian film history, as its success encouraged official sponsorship of the "art" cinema which began the Indian "New Wave." This time set in Gujarat and made in Hindi, it tells the story of an "honest" bureaucrat whose colonial values are undermined by one of Sen's most charming characters — an unsophisticated village girl.

National Film Theatre (U.K.) **brochure Mrinal Sen Retrospective October/November 1980**

AAKALER SANDHANEY
(In Search of Famine)

The director (left) waits as his actress applies make-up before they film their version of the Bengal famine.

1980/Col/125 mins/Bengali
Direction/Screenplay
Mrinal Sen
Produced by
Dhiresh Chakraborty
Story
Amalendu Chakraborty
Camera
K. K. Mahajan
Editing
Gangadhar Naskar
Music
Salil Chowdhury
Art Direction
Suresh Chandra Chandra
Players
*Dhritiman Chatterjee
(Director), Smita Patil
(Actress/village
woman), Sreela Majumdar
(village woman),
Dipankar Dev (Film star),
Rajen Tarafdar (villager),
Radhamohan Bhattacharya
(schoolteacher)*
Enquiries.
*D. K. Films Enterprise,
P 36 India Exchange Place,
Calcutta 700 001.
Tel: 265985/265986*

Aakaler Sandhaney begins with a film unit arriving at Samra Bazar, a rural settlement, a two-hour drive away from Calcutta, to shoot a film based on the famine of 1943. The intention of the unit is to re-enact the old tragedy. They discover instead that famine in the countryside of Bengal is an ever-present reality. The interaction between the members of the film crew and the villagers generates a series of escalating tensions. The film unit is forced to abandon the shooting and retreat to the security of the make-believe world of film studios.

As the film unit arrives an old villager remarks ironically, "The city people have come to take pictures of the famine," to which another villager retorts, "The famine! It is written all over us." The difference between the actual tragedy and its intellectual appreciation has been stated; the problem of communication has been raised.

The unit members busy themselves with settling down in the decaying but still beautiful house called Vishal Bari. They worry over lack of electricity and toilet facilities and details of their menu which the production manager is expected to arrange. In the process a new urban island is created which has nothing in common with the surrounding ocean of rural humanity.

The members of the film unit become almost totally confined to their own fantasy world. But the island cannot remain isolated from the "other people." It extends to the vegetable market where the bulk purchases for the film unit push up prices. The empty packets of expensive cigarettes discarded by the director are greedily picked up by the children, and his "cut, cut" noisily imitated by them. Finally, a search is made for a suitable local girl to replace one of the actresses who has thrown a tantrum and left.

It is the last act of unthinking and arrogant intrusion into the social fabric of the village which finally leads to a confrontation. The role involved is that of a prostitute. The film director in his impatient urban wisdom is unable to comprehend the stigma that will be attached to any village girl who performs this role.

The village in turn visits the "island" to watch the shooting or serve as menials for the unit. There is Haren, the weaver, who had joined a theatre company as a boy, starting with female roles and graduating to others over a period of thirty years. The times have changed and he now feels a bit lost. He thinks he has found a kindred soul, a fellow artist, in the director.

Aakaler Sandhaney has been woven out of a wide variety of thematic threads: the patronising attitude of the urban educated towards the village folk, the dehumanising presence of a starvation level of existence, and the desperate choice which it inflicts upon its victims.

The obsessive love of the farmer for his land and the machinations of landlords and contractors to rob the farmer of his land are analysed alongside the twilight tragedy of a feudal family in decay and the loneliness of an old woman chained to a husband slowly dying of paralysis.

The world of Haren or the village woman Durga and her husband, the old school teacher and other village folk, is only dimly perceived by the director and his unit. They hardly seem to notice the parallel between their fictional story of Savitri being enacted by Smita Patil and the real life of Durga.

In two anguished passages, the recreation of Savitri's life in 1943 is transformed into the real life of Durga in 1980. Through similar parallels, the film provides a probing, sarcastic comment on social attitudes towards cinema as compared to theatre, the ethics of film making, and finally, the hollowness of a film director's "commitment."

Kunwar Bikram Singh
Filmfare,
May, 1981

The fascinating charm of this film within a film story lies in the inter-cutting of several levels of yesterday and today, of urban and rural mentalities, of conflicts between the film people and the local population described with a satirical undertone. *In Search of Famine* belongs among the most exciting films of our days.

Edmund Luft
Allegemeine Zeitung
January 28, 1981

Filmography

1956 **RAAT BHORE (Night's End)**
B&W/114 mins/Bengali
Lead players: Manik Chatterjee, Chhabi Biswas
A poor village boy inter-relates with a rich urban family.

1959 **NEEL AKASHER NEECHEY (Under the Blue Sky)**
B&W/120 mins/Bengali
Lead players: Kali Bannerjee, Manju Dey
The story of a poor Chinese salesman living a dreary life in Calcutta in the early thirties when both India and China had been fighting Imperial expansion in different political equations.

1960 **BAISHEY SRAVANA (The Wedding Day)**
B&W/110 mins/Bengali
Lead players: Madhabi Mukherjee, Jnanesh Mukherjee
During the Bengal famine of '43, a middle-aged village hawker marries a lovely sixteen-year-old girl who initially revives his drab life. The famine causes the marriage and the fabric of village life to end in disaster. In this early film, Sen explores the socio-economic causes of poverty.

1961 **PUNNASCHA (Over Again)**
B&W/120 mins/Bengali
Lead players: Soumitra Chatterjee, Kanika Majumdar, N. Vishwanathan
Urban family relationships form the central theme. A woman's shift from the traditional, domestic role of wife to that of contributor to the family income by taking a job, hurls the woman and her husband against each other.

1962 **ABASHESHEY (And at Last)**
B&W/120 mins/Bengali
Lead players: Sabitri Chatterjee, Asit Baran
A farce on divorce, Indian style.

1964 **PROTINIDHI (Two plus One)**
B&W/120 mins/Bengali
Lead players: Soumitra Chatterjee, Sabitri Chatterjee.
A modern young man meets a young widow and soon they grow intimate. The innocent child of the woman by her previous husband poses a problem. In a society where taboos play a dominant role, the marital life of the protagonists grows increasingly difficult and finally collapses.

1965 **AKASH KUSUM (Up in the Clouds)**
B&W/110 mins/Bengali
Lead players:Soumitra Chatterjee, Sudhendu Chatterjee, Aparna Sen
Trying for success in the competitive Calcutta business

world, a young man desperately tries to break the wealth barrier by marriage. He succeeds in compromising himself and is finally humiliated. For Sen, the film's modernity lies less in its theme than in its style. The film sparked off a debate about its use of Indian politics in cinema.

1967 MATIRA MANISHA (Two Brothers)
B&W/120 mins/Bengali
Lead players: Sarat Pujari, Prasanta Nanda, Sujata
Working outside Bengal, Sen sets this film in Orissa. The film contrasts traditional and modern values as exemplified by the different attitudes of two brothers to their inherited land, representing an effort to break free from the archetypal film image of rural India.

1969 BHUVAN SHOME

1970 ICHHAPURAN (Wish Fulfilment)
Col/70 mins/Bengali and Hindi versions
Lead players: Raju, Sadhu Meher, Shekhar Chatterjee
Producer: Children's Film Society.
The comic and absurd fantasy of an estranged father and his young son whose ages are transposed by the goddess of wish fulfilment. They revert to their original age, wiser and happier.

1971 EK ADHURI KAHANI (An Unfinished Story)
B&W/110 mins/Bengali
Lead players: Utpal Dutt, Shekhar Chatterjee,
Bulbul Mukherjee
A middle class outsider starts a new job as a cashier in a sugar mill located in an agricultural area. He exposes the previously obscured ruthlessness of the boss towards the workers, and sets off a common struggle, often confused and violent, of workers and farmers against exploitation.

INTERVIEW
B&W/87 mins/Bengali
Lead Players: Ranjit Mullick, Bulbul Mukherjee
The first of Sen's *Calcutta Trilogy* covering his more overtly political phase. A young man loses a job opportunity because he cannot obtain a suit for the interview. The film is a pointed attack on the vestiges of colonial attitudes, and an attempt at liberating cinema from the confines of narrative structure and logic.

1972 CALCUTTA '71
Col/132 mins/Bengali
Lead players: Ranjit Mullick. Utpal Dutt, Geeta Sen
Agit-prop and resolutely non-naturalist, this film recounts five separate incidents spread over forty years with the common theme of poverty and exploitation, linked by an imagined, timeless figure who by 1971 has come both to understand exploitation and know how to take direct action.

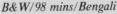

1973 PADATIK (The Guerrilla Fighter)
B&W/98 mins/Bengali
Lead players: Dhritiman Chatterjee, Simi Garewal
The third part of the *Calcutta Trilogy* concentrates on an
individual, a political "extremist" who breaks out of police
custody and is sheltered by a woman who herself has
defied society's conventions by living independently.
Although loyal, he questions the policies of the Party,
realising instances where leadership is wanting.

1974 CHORUS
B&W/126 mins/Bengali
Lead players: Utpal Dutt, Geeta Sen, Shekhar Chatterjee
The film begins like a fairy tale with the gods creating
a hundred jobs for the people. Unfortunately thousands
queue for them. Popular discontent is mobilised as word
spreads that this is just another trick. The Chorus, as well
as performing the traditional role of story teller, provides
the political message, juxtaposing stylisation and caricature
with neo-realist and documentary sequences and direct
address to camera.

1976 MRIGAYA (The Royal Hunt)
Col/110 mins/Hindi
Lead players: Mithun Chakravorty, Mamta Shankar
The film is a reminder of the skill in story-telling and the
sly humour which Sen had tended to repress in the
rigorous, politically committed *Calcutta Trilogy*. The film
deals with a historical event (the Santhal Revolt of 1901)
in which a tribal hunter becomes a revolutionary hero.
Though the film is not strictly allegorical, parallels with
political situations are clear.

1977 OKA OORIE KATHA (The Outsiders)
Col/115 mins/Telugu
*Lead players: Vasudeva Rao, Mamta Shankar,
Narayana Rao*
A masterly political parable, set in a Southern Indian
State, tells the story of a half-mad peasant who refuses
to work any more, declaring "To work in this rotten
system is to serve the system." His son marries a young
girl who works as a labourer. She dies in childbirth. Father
and son beg money for her cremation but squander it
on drink.

1978 PARASHURAM (Man with the Axe)
Col/99 mins/Bengali
*Lead players: Arun Mukherjee, Biswas Chakraborty,
Nirmal Ghosh*
Parashuram is a mythical hero who avenged his father's
death by raising his axe twenty-one times. This "man with
the axe" is slightly different, an ordinary rural migrant
moving among slum dwellers, living in fear of authority
and petty criminals. Only in fantasy can he revolt and

confront all his enemies. The film blends contemporary social reality and the imaginative traditions of popular oral literature and fairground entertainers.

1979 EK DIN PRATIDIN (And Quiet Rolls the Dawn)

Col/95 mins/Bengali
Lead players: Geeta Sen, Mamta Shankar, Sreela Mazumdar
The theme is the decline and fall of the Calcutta petite bourgeoisie. The film is set in the ramshackle tenement of a rambling old house. One of its families has a young girl as the only breadwinner. She remains away at work one night into the early hours. The family's concern shifts to fear of impropriety and loss of reputation. They blame the girl. The film demonstrates the disintegration of a class.

1980 AAKALER SANDHANEY (In Search of Famine)

Smita Patil at twenty-five is clearly the queen of Indian parallel cinema, as much an icon for filmmakers of this milieu as Anna Karina was for young directors in France at the outset of the New Wave. She began her career as a television announcer and was discovered by Shyam Benegal, who gave her a start in films. Patil is not a classic beauty, but the lady glows. She never makes a false move on screen.

Elliott Stein
Film Comment (U.S.A.)
July 1981

1981 CHAALCHITRA (The Kaleidoscope)

(Under Production)
Col/approx. 100 mins/Bengali
Lead players: Anjan Dutt, Geeta Sen, Utpal Dutt
An enthusiastic, intelligent young man is asked by an editor to try his hand at a news story. With an eye at getting a reporter's job, the man sets about his task with such zeal that he cannot do justice to it. He tries every trick he knows to no avail. He literally has a nightmare on the job. The editor then asks him to do a serious piece with a social message. The aspiring journalist lands the job without time to think of its repercussions on his conscience.

1967 MOVING PERSPECTIVES (documentary)

KUMAR SHAHANI

Kumar Shahani is without doubt the most vigorous of the young Indian film makers, on the plane of his thinking as on the plane of his cinema.

Henri Micciollo
Cinema 75 (France)

"The most outstanding event of the season was our introduction to the work of Kumar Shahani. His *Maya Darpan*, superbly and sensitively photographed in colour, marks him out as the most talented Indian director to appear since Ray. If other directors are successfully copying avant garde techniques from the West, Shahani alone displays the originality of genius. The film is not easy. Shahani lacks Ray's popular appeal and may therefore find it harder to make his mark. But if luck is on his side we should hear much more of him."

Thus wrote the British critic, Mansell Stimpson in 'Film' when a season of New Indian Cinema opened at the National Film Theatre in London in 1973. His words were oddly prophetic. Despite the lavish praise bestowed on Shahani's first feature abroad, it has remained the only film he has ever completed. *Maya Darpan* has never had a single commercial screening in India, a country which makes the largest number of movies in the world.

"I was surprised at the hostility to my film here," recalls Shahani, who is now 40. "I tried to make a simple story within a lyrical framework." Critics panned it for its excessively slow pace ("Nothing happens!", they complained), the repetitiveness of some shots, for being altogether too obscure.

And yet, for anyone who was prepared to open himself to the film, it was a revelation. Henri Micciollo, then the director of the Alliance Francaise in Bombay, wrote to point out how Shahani rejected "all elements of change: one could say that everything — the framing, the positioning of colours, the sounds — acquires significance. This universe of signs demands of the spectator an active participation . . . "

Shahani uses form and space and colour to convey how the life and spirit of a young girl, Taran, is confined by her aloof and authoritarian father, living in a crumbling mansion. The high degree of stylisation — with which he tries to convey the oppression of the girl — was found stifling by viewers.

In an interview some years ago, the director said: "I am against using characters as puppets or gadgets or just for graphic purposes. I know there are some other film makers who do it, but if you observe the way I have taken certain shots, they are extremely lengthy.

"For example, in Taran's room, the camera follows her doing apparently insignificant things, registering the slightest movements. Graphic elements are most important. But when one is using actual actors, life bursts through the graphics."

Another criticism against the film was that it was too "European" in its sensibility. This has obviously something to do with Shahani's sojourn in Paris with IDHEC (Institute of Higher Studies in Cinema), and more specifically, his working on a film with Bresson (he even appear briefly in *Une Femme Douce)*.

"I have never understood this," confesses Shahan When he showed the film to Bresson — without subtitles - the famous French director said he could never imagine film so slow; an occidental could never have made i (One must recall the general Western reaction to the "slo pace" of life in the Orient: wasn't it Truffaut who declare as he walked out of Ray's trail-blazing first film, *Pathe Panchali* (The Song of the Road), "Pad, pad, pad, throug the paddy fields!") While Bresson found *Maya Darpa* visually beautiful, "what intrigued him most was th rhythm. He would shut his eyes to see where the sh would end, beating his palm on his thigh," recalls Shahan

"I find two kinds of reactions," says the directo "There are those who expected certain things — poverty o metaphysics — and were disappointed. Others took to it i a big way. But even among the admirers, there is som hesitation, a crass attitude which seems to doubt whethe such work can be done in an underdeveloped country A BBC man, when the film was shown in London, fo instance, said he could't quite think where, but he ha seen the same use of colour before. When I questione him closely, he couldn't come up with it! In the sam way, Mani Kaul's use of volume has never bee acknowledged in the West."

At home, the Film Finance Corporation (now merge into the National Film Development Corporation or NFDC came under severe attack for putting what was rhetorical termed "taxpayers money" into a venture of this kind A personal statement was a mere indulgence in a countr like India, they said. Others saw in it an experiment whic deserved to be encouraged because it would give youn film makers in the country an idea of how the languag of cinema can be extended and refined. Shahani is paine to think that he isn't treated as a film maker in his ow right, but as some kind of innovator, if not the mento of other struggling directors.

"Ever since I have made the film, I am being constantl grilled about it and am put on the defensive," he admits "Objectively, the severe reaction has set me back. Th FFC wouldn't easily consider financing another film. Bu I was against the avant-gardist position from the ver beginning; it was never my intention to do this becaus it is an effete pre-occupation."

Shahani's second film, *Tarang* (Wave), has been stuc halfway through its shooting because of some financia problems. "The film deals with an industrial family, founde by the head who made a fortune in the last war throug unscrupulous means." It is obviously an easier plot tha *Maya Darpan* and he wanted big names from the Hind film industry in the cast. Trying his best not to let thes reverses get him down, Shahani hopes that things wil sort themselves out.

He, along with Mani Kaul, has been among th brightest alumni of the Film Institute in Pune, from where h graduated in 1966. He was attracted to the film making course—still the only professional one in the country—after being exposed to features as a member of a Bombay film society. At Pune, he recalls the presence of Ritwik Ghatak, a controversial film maker and teacher, known as much for his charisma as for the chaos in his personal life (he died of alcoholism a few years ago). "He prevented dilettantism," Shahani points out. The other influence was the great Indian polymath, D. D. Kosambi, who taught the young man how to look "at oneself at one's own people," drawing not only on history but also archeology and even numismatics.

Shahani has not made very many documentaries, but he attends to them with the same painstaking rigour with which he approaches a feature film. "I am horrified that most people one meets do no research when they make films!" he exclaims. "For them, there seems to be nothing wrong in leaving things to chance."

After he stood first in his course at Pune, he won a French government scholarship to IDHEC in Paris, where he spent most of the time at the Cinematheque, seeing three or four films a day. He opted for courses in Western music and was a keen observer of the cataclysmic events of May 1968 in France.

Six years after making his first feature, he conducted a study on the theory and practice of the epic form, on a scholarship from an Indian industrial house. If things work out, he may well put this knowledge to use in a film made with help from the West Bengal government, even taking episodes straight out of the 'Mahabharata', India's ancient epic. During his study, he learned Sanskrit to enable him to read plays and texts in their original.

The same fervour drove Shahani and his wife Roshan to learn classical Indian music from a teacher some years ago. Another plan is to make a film on a tradition which has sustained much of North Indian music over the past three centuries.

Shahani acknowledges the "close collaboration" of Roshan, who also worked on the script of *Tarang* and has been a strong support. They have a daughter named Uttara.

Darryl d'Monte

A slight frail frame, a finely drawn face with probing eyes, a charming smile and a shock of unruly hair make Shahani look like a poet. He is one of the most respected intellectuals of cinema in India. His scholarly papers on myth and cinema and on Ghatak have been widely published. He is also a regular guest lecturer at Pune's Film Institute, a favourite with the students because his erudition is free from pedantry, whether he is talking of the epic form or the esoteric intricacies of classical music. He made a persuasive compere on Bombay TV in his educative weekly program called 'Montage' which informed a generally disinterested public on the finer points of film aesthetics.

MAYA DARPAN

Taran, defiant and yet in awe of her father, who is a stern traditionalist.

1972/Col/105 mins/Hindi
Direction/Produced by
Kumar Shahani
Screenplay
Nirmal Verma
Camera
K. K. Mahajan
Music
Bhaskar Chandavarkar
Editing
Madhu Sinha
Art Direction
Bansi Chandragupta
Players
Aditi (Taran), Anil Pandya
(engineer babu), Kanta Vyas
(aunt), Anil Kaul (Dewan sahib).
Enquiries
Kumar Shahani Productions,
37 Shankar Mahal,
Sophia College Lane,
Bombay 400 026.
Tel: 824983

We pass through old dusty corridors of a house in the Indo-British style, searching for life behind the yellow ochre and charred walls, opening doors of brown wood. We discover a woman in red and black on a tattered white sheet, the colours suggesting the recurrent Kali motif of fertility and change (Kali is a traditional Indian goddess worshipped as mother, creator and destroyer. She is both tender and fierce). Taran is the young daughter of a former functionary of a small principality, who has lost her mother in her adolescence. Taran is still unmarried. Her brother, after a quarrel with the father, has left for Assam where he works on a tea estate. He often writes to her and she dreams of escaping from the dust, the heat, the oppression of the old house to the lush landscape of the hills.

It is only her attachment to her obstinate father, an unconscious one, which prevents her from leaving. Her only consolation is the tenderness that she receives from the old widowed aunt, who is also the link with the past. Her father's refusal to get her married into a family with the necessary status has wasted her youth and has created an unbearable guilt in him. The exposition is worked out in reds and yellows which find their resolution in blue — her vision of herself as the secularised icon of Kali. The reference is reiterated by the lullaby on the sound track.

The change and violence, constant factors in her environment, begin to mean something to her when, mutedly, she feels the possibility of change in herself. She grows restless. She dreams of the horrors of war and the empire and the valiant spirit of those who fight in the struggle for independence, jumbling images of historical documents of India and of present-day industry and Vietnam.

She is intrigued and attracted by a young man (a city-bred engineer) who represents a rational determination to fight the blind forces of nature. His mundane, business-like attitude evokes in her a sense of freedom. But, he quotes Friedrich Engels in the film, "Freedom is the recognition of necessity." It is imperative for her to understand not only her individual predicament but also the necessity of change in history. And her responsibility is to make her father accept this necessity and at the same time, on the personal level, to give him all the tenderness he needs. But until the end of the film, he appears to her only as an oppressive figure. Once she realises her father's helplessness, she responds with love and decides to assert herself. Now, she is both fierce and tender, objectively. She realises in action what is suggested earlier as merely an internal vision of herself (the blue icon).

She rejects the utopia of Assam. She accepts her father for what he is and decides to stay back and look after him. She begins to build a relationship with the engineer. She plunges into the life around her, becomes part of the community of people who build the new society with their hands and their consciousness.

Once again we return to the red, black and white colours with a defiant drumbeat. Finally, we come to the cool but neutral landscape which is now accessible to us, as is the new life to her, freeing her both from a romantic dream and the feudal oppression that had nurtured it.

A NOTE ON COLOUR
In *Maya Darpan*, the whole action — and not merely emotional equivalences — is worked out in colour. The basic element of progression of content is treated through the colour axis. The broad movement is from red to green, which are qualitative opposites. The exposition is done through a tension created by red and yellow. The intensity of red is internalised and contrasted against the extension qualities of yellow. There is an explosion of yellow in the newsreel sequence and finally the tension is resolved by the introduction of the blue body of the woman — a secularised reference to the traditional Indian image of a mother goddess. Orange, the natural opposite of blue, now takes over. It is broken up again into red and yellow and both achieve their own almost monochromatic purity in different sequences of the film. Yellow, with merging forms, fading into white is counterpointed against Taran's

Taran caught between tradition and change.

He uses colour beautifully and has a real gift for telling a story through tension and atmosphere rather than through over-obvious plotting.

Derek Malcolm
The Guardian (U.K.)
January 22, 1976

173

sensing of life within her. Red, towards the end of the film, in stark combination with black and white brings us back to the fertility principle and to the main colour movement of the film. This time, there is a straight transition to green but once again providing a counterpoint through the emptiness of the landscape.

Within the scene, it is the change of volumes and tints and the lack of resolution between two colours that sets the movement — and not the introduction of a new psychological colour component. There are no one-to-one equivalences of content and colour. Each colour changes its meaning with each new juxtaposition of gestures, sound, movement, another colour or a repetition, after a certain sequence of events.

Bua, the widowed aunt, who sees everything but can do nothing.

Filmography

1966: **THE GLASS PANE** (short)
B & W/10 mins
Student diploma film about a couple who come back from a funeral, unable to relate to each other or their surroundings.

1967: **MANMAD PASSENGER** (short)
B & W/15 mins
About a young man trying to search for something to commit himself to.

1970: **RAILS FOR THE ROAD** (documentary)
Col/10 mins
An export promotion film for Hindustan Steel Ltd.

1971: **OBJECT** (short)
Col/10 mins/16 mn
Made for a psychoanalyst's thesis, about a patient's fantasies regarding potency symbols.

1972: **MAYA DARPAN**

1973: **FIRE IN THE BELLY** (documentary)
B & W/18 mins
About the drought in Maharashtra and a rhythm of hunger clearly sensed.

Under Production
Currently directing his second feature film *Tarang* (Wave). The film deals with the tensions of a modern industrial family in an epic way. The founder of the business has made money unscrupulously during the war. The son-in-law is the entrepreneurial type while the Oxbridge educated nephew is more interested in foreign collaboration.
Lead Players: Amol Palekar, Smita Patil and Shreeram Lagoo.

Shahani is planning to make a film based on the 'Mahabharata'. The film will deal with fratricidal conflict on an epic social scale, which as a characteristic of contemporary Indian society, found its most poignant expression in Bengal between 1969 and 1973.

A documentary on the Gwalior school of North Indian classical music is under consideration which will adapt the manner of history known to India for centuries — as fact embedded in legend.

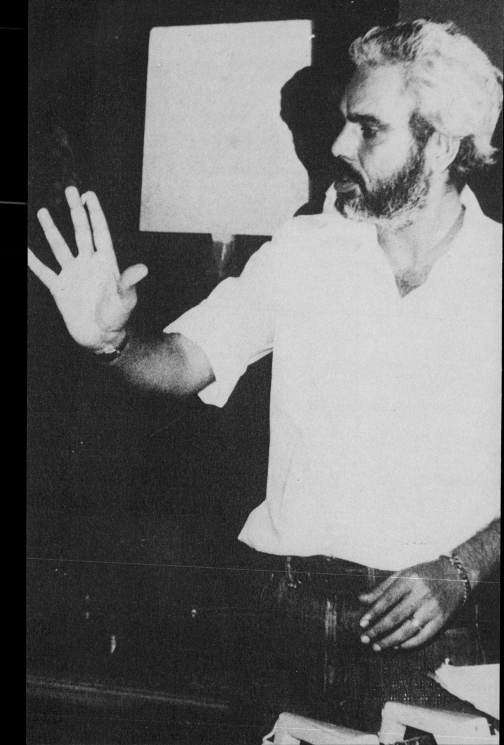

SURINDER SURI

Thirty-five year old Surinder Suri has a deceptive young-old appearance ... premature white hair, a well-trimmed beard, streaked with grey that is at variance with his youthful eyes, bright with curiosity. The face crinkles into a smile when he is taken to be much older. Suri frankly counts it an advantage — the implied experience of added years may impress producers.

"I made the film to satisfy the child in me," declares Suri, the Indian associate director of *Rikki Tikki Tavi* (The Brave Mongoose). It was an unexpected bonanza for a young man just out of the Film Institute in 1974. The shared gold medal for Best Student Film made an impression on the establishment.

Suri, with the rest of the unit, had to run the entire bureaucratic gamut of co-production hassles — including the impounding of the cobras (the villains in the film) by airport authorities for not having valid papers. Despite minor flaws of dubbing and lip synchronisation, the film is visually striking. It captures the elusive whimsical charm of Kipling's story. The script fleshes out the barely suggested human characters in the original. Much of the credit for retaining the period flavour goes to Suri. He vetoed transposing Kipling to modern times. It would break the illusion.

Zaguridi, the veteran Russian director, was in overall command and he supervised the film. The Russian had to learn the nuances of colonial India during Kipling's own time, the turn of the century. The behaviour pattern of the animals, the real stars of the story, was unfamiliar. The animals and their folklore are indigenous to India.

Suri speaks with admiration for the eighty-two-year-old Zaguridi, energetic and full of a rare passion. The unit called him "grandpa" in affection. Earlier, he had directed the first co-production of the Children's Film Society, *Black Mountain,* "exclusively and exquisitely" according to Suri.

East or West, entertainment satisfies the eternal child in man. This is Suri's credo as he cites the dormant appeal of nostalgia in support. He enjoyed directing the children. "They are plastic material. No professional can match the natural performance given so intuitively." It was the mongoose, with its low IQ that posed problems. Professional snake charmers were found useless. They finally located an old magician in a village near Pune who succeeded in transforming one among the three aspirants into a biddable star. Pampering and overfeeding by the unit led to an ungainly girth, endangering the sprightly young mongoose image.

Normally soft-spoken, Suri has scathing comments on the usual run of "wishy-washy films palmed off on children." Conventional fairy tales do not satisfy the urge for adventure, and ignore their increasing sophistication The gore and glamour of the Hindi multi-starrer has percolated even into remote villages. "Don't treat them as mentally retarded," is his plea. Asked why he did not make more children's films, Suri's rejoinder is "What else are the 450 films we turn out every year?" For all this gentle derision, Suri is not apologetic about making commercial films. He is precise about the ideas he wants to work into the formula.

Ahsaas (Experience) was his first independent film. Suri was not successful in emphasising the generation gap in what was basically a teenage love story but conveyed the intense need of the young for communication. The film exploited their sexual discovery of each other and so earned an Adult Certificate. He shrugs off the disappointment: perhaps the Censors are "used to vulgarity, not realism." *Ahsaas* is remembered for its expressive song picturisation.

Suri advances his own justification for the inevitable songs in our films. He points out that folk theatre all over India uses song as an integral part of the medium. Not only is it the much required "breather," but offers, says Suri, "an escape from the graph of the narrative." He commends the maturity of Indian audiences for their readiness to accept stylisation via song.

Beneath the modest demeanour, one senses a quiet tenacity. He talks with undisguised enthusiasm about the current film *Naya Johnny* (New Johnny). Within the format of the spy thriller he wants to bring out the strange subtle bond that grows between the hunter and his prey. Almost like the Hemingway hero, a sense of exclusive identification evolves through living the other's life in the imagination.

It is yet to be seen how he succeeds in translating these ideas into the framework of the Bombay-formula film. In the invidious world of commercial cinema, a hit is all that counts. One wonders how Suri, with a penchant for describing "the feel of the narrative" will come to terms with it.

A certain restlessness beneath the surface placidity is discernible. Even during his Film Institute days, boredom drove him to invest in a 16 mm camera and freelance for the nascent TV, shooting newsreel footage. As a student in Delhi, he had no interest either in the stage or films. He confesses, "I was a backbencher and understood their problems." Only the visiting spectacular Ice Show attracted him to the performing arts. It was the unexciting amateur stage scene that led him to join the Film Institute in 1971.

Perhaps the subconscious choice was made earlier. As a child he was fascinated by the projection room of the family-owned theatre in a small town called Sirsa. He ran it during vacations. He recalls that he was more interested in the audience reaction than the images on the screen. It is full circle back to his childhood, the frequently reiterated faith in the child in man.

Maithili Rao

RIKKI TIKKI TAVI
(The Brave Mongoose)

Arch enemies, snake and mongoose, battling over a question of loyalty and devotion.

*1977/Colour/75 mins/Hindi
and Russian versions*
Direction
A. Zaguridi
Produced by
Children's Film Society
Associate Director
Surinder Suri
Script
*Based on a story by Rudyard
Kipling*
Camera
Riipeko V. Pestvalik
Music
A. Sintake
Players
*Alexei Batalov (The father)
Alexsitiv (Teddy)
Sandeep Vishnu (John)
Surinder Suri (Mr. Chibnell)
Margaret (The mother)*
Enquiries
*Children's Film Society,
Hingorani House,
78, Dr. Annie Besant Road,
Worli,
Bombay 400 018.
Tel: 379302/377478*

In true 'Jungle Book' style, Kipling tells the story through the enquiring eyes of a lively young mongoose. The human characters, just sketched, have been filled out. The British element in this version is tinged with a Russian atmosphere, since its foreign actors are all Russian.

The setting is a British forest officer's bungalow at the edge of a forest teeming with animal life. It is colonial India at the turn of the century. Teddy, the English boy is playing truant in the forest, along with his Indian companion. He is familiar with the natural habitat of the animals..

It is spring. The nesting birds, the elephants sporting in the water, the tigress with her cubs, make the forest come alive. The quick and curious young of the mongoose are at play when danger strikes. A sudden heavy rain causes a dam to burst and the river is in spate.

Teddy notices a young mongoose desperately struggling to clamber to the safety of a rock. He rescues it, braving the surging deluge, only to find that his benumbed legs cannot carry him. His friend summons help. Teddy's legs are paralysed and he is confined to a wheel chair. The father and son care deeply for animals; the bedraggled mongoose thrives to the chagrin of the distraught mother.

The mongoose, christened Rikki Tikki (in imitation of its war cry) is Teddy's sole companion. Chibnell, the family friend, takes him out for a ride once in a while.

Running around the garden Rikki Tikki confronts the big black cobra, *Nag,* his arch enemy. *Nag* and his scheming wife *Nagaina* plan to kill all the older inmates of the big sprawling house, so that their soon-to-arrive young will have undisturbed peace. Their reasoning: the mongoose will go back to the wilderness when the family is decimated.

Overhearing the plot, Rikki Tikki faces the cobra who

179

Teddy (right) with Chibnell, the understanding adult.

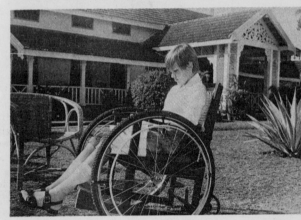

Teddy, paralysed and confined to a wheel-chair after his rescue mission.

is lying in wait for the master of the house. As the midnight battle rages in the bathroom and on to the living room, the noise of tumbling utensils wakes Teddy's father and he shoots the cobra.

Next, the relentless Rikki, destroys the eggs of *Nagaina* due to hatch any moment. The enraged widow pursues her enemy to the garden where Teddy is asleep in his wheel chair. The heroism of his pet mongoose and his own apprehension of danger act as catalysts. Teddy stands on his feet just as Rikki eliminates the dangerous cobra forever.

Maithili Rao

Filmography

1977 RIKKI TIKKI TAVI

1978 AHSAAS (Experience)
Col/135 mins/Hindi
Lead players: Parvez, Dina, Kiran Vairale and
Rakesh Bedi.
A story of young lovers in affluent, cosmopolitan Bombay. The rival parents are opposed to their marriage and are typically nouveau riche in their derogatory contempt for successful competitors. The teenage girl is pregnant and they run away to a deserted house in idyllic countryside. The new-born baby and grandmotherly family attendant bring about the reconciliation.

Suri on the sets of Naya Johnny, *directing India's "evergreen" hero, Dev Anand (left).*

NAYA JOHNNY (New Johnny)
Lead players: Dev Anand, Hema Malini and
Shammi Kapoor.
An ambitious forthcoming film based on Suri's story. A spy thriller that attempts to convey the complex psychological bond that grows between the pursuer and the pursued.

MATLABI (The Selfish One)
Lead players: Girish Karnad, Raj Kiran and Anita Raj.
Intended to be an exploration of the basic irony of the situation — a custodian of law developing immunity to its sanctions as a result of his own special position. He finds it temptingly easy to circumvent the law.

An untitled new venture, again based on Suri's story, is an unusual triangle of an adolescent boy growing up in an all-masculine household, a sympathetic woman teacher only a few years older, and the silent crush a classmate has on the boy. The possessiveness of the boy compels the teacher to leave the small town.

181

BANSI CHANDRAGUPTA

Art director ... who created a world as real as it was imaginary

A generation after Bansi Chandragupta built in the authenticity for Jean Renoir's *La Fleuve* (1950), he helped the young Bombay cineastes realise their dreams on the screen. It is said that he alone, of the team that made *Pather Panchali* (Song of the Road), had any previous cinematographic experience. It was not unusual for Bansi to find himself in that place again in the seventies, with directors and cameramen making their first films.

Bansi was the perfect technician. He could disagree with you fundamentally but his work ethic always drove him to the most impeccable detailing of what the style of the film demanded.

With Satyajit Ray and Subroto Mitra, Bansi had perfected the art of creating a perfect illusion of reality. But, by its very nature, it was a self-effacing art.

No-one recognised Bansi Chandragupta's sets as his creations. Most often their authenticity was attributed to shooting on real locations. *Pather Panchali* was mistaken for a documentary in the tradition of Flaherty. A recent film with the backdrop of slums in Bombay, *Chakra* (The Vicious Circle) was claimed to be shot in the lower depths of this festering city.

I know of few technicians who could recognise the magnificent recreation of *Jalsaghar* (The Music Room). It was only when Satyajit Ray's and Subroto Mitra's camera became more mobile, in *Charulata* and *Nayak* (The Hero) that Bansi Chandragupta's contribution was perceived.

Yet in the city that he lived, the city of his adoption, Calcutta, he could not subsist. He shifted to Bombay, as reluctant as a debutant in the fantasy world of its studios, but warm, friendly, modest with all the young film makers, cameramen, recordists, art-directors who surrounded him. The tycoons of Bombay's mass film industry would dub him expensive and finicky. He would spray salt in the air, they would say, if a set were to represent a location by the sea! It was the younger lot of people who adopted him, teased him for being so self-effacing, drew him out, challenged the presumptions that have hounded Indian Cinema since neo-realism visited us. We discovered that he greatly admired the German expressionist experiment.

Hidden somewhere in his mind was an idea of a feature film that would, in a radically different way from the expressionists, work from the sets, from an exclosure.

Bansi had left his home long ago. He created from his nostalgia, a world as real as it was imaginary.

I do not know how we will ever reconcile our imagination to this loss: Bansi's death in a distant place on June 27, 1981.

Kumar Shahani

Notes on Contributors

U. R. Ananthamurthy is a Kannada novelist and professor of English.

Santi P. Chowdhury is a documentary film maker and a director on the Board of the National Film Development Corporation.

Peter Colaco is Managing Director, Marketing Consultants and Agencies Ltd., Bangalore.

Uma da Cunha is film critic for *Financial Express.*

Darryl d'Monte has worked as Resident Editor of the *Indian Express,* Bombay and as Editor of the Sunday Magazine Section of the *Times of India.*

Anil Dharkar is the editor of *Debonair,* a fortnightly.

Gopal Dutt teaches and writes on film.

B. D. Garga is a film critic and documentary film maker.

Shanta Gokhale is a freelance writer.

Nirmal Goswami is a Director of Ulka Advertising.

Shama Habibullah is a documentary film maker.

Attia Hosain is a novelist.

Siddharth Kak is the Managing Editor of *Cinema Vision,* a quarterly.

M. V. Kamath is the Editor of the *Illustrated Weekly of India.*

Satti Khanna is a research scholar and teaches Indian cinema in the department of South and South East Asia Studies, University of California, Berkeley.

Arun Khopkar makes documentary films and lectures on film.

V. Sasikumar is the Bombay correspondent of the Malayalam weekly, *Kalakaumudi.*

V. K. Madhavan Kutty is the Delhi correspondent of the Malayalam weekly *Matrubhoomi.*

Iqbal Masud is film critic for *Sunday Standard.*

Vinod Mehta is the Editor of the *Sunday Observer.*

Amitabha Mukherjee is a research scholar at the Tata Institute of Fundamental Research.

D. G. Nadkarni is a theatre, film and art critic.

Rohini Nilekani works for *Bombay,* a fortnightly.

Xanthe Noble is a textile designer.

Pearl Padamsee works in theatre and films and is an actress.

Mubarak Pasricha is Film Executive, Lintas India Ltd.

Saidan Puri is a pseudonym.

Ashish Rajadhyaksha is a freelance journalist.

J. S. Rao works for the Bombay newspaper, *Free Press Journal.*

Maithili Rao is film critic for *Free Press Bulletin.*

Arun Sachdev writes on the arts.

Kumar Shahani is a film maker, writer nad lecturer on film.

Bikram Singh is Director of Films with the Ministry of Information and Broadcasting.

Shama Zaidi is a script writer and art director.

Acknowledgements

Film India: an exhibition organized by The Asia Society, The Museum of Modern Art in New York, and the Directorate of Film Festivals—New Delhi, with the cooperation of the Indo-U.S. Subcommission on Education and Culture.

The exhibition is co-directed by Muriel Peters, Director, Department of Film and Broadcasting, The Asia Society; Adrienne Mancia, Curator, Department of Film, The Museum of Modern Art; Raghunath Raina, Director, Directorate of Film Festivals; and Erik Barnouw, Director, Motion Picture, Broadcasting, and Recorded Sound Division, The Library of Congress; with the assistance of Larry Kardish, Associate Curator, The Museum of Modern Art.

For their generous and enthusiastic assistance and support we extend out sincere appreciation to: Air India, the National Endowment of the Humanities, the Indian Council for Cultural Relations, the National Film Archive of India, Pune, the Asian Cultural Council, the Smithsonian Institution Foreign Currency Program, and the National Film Development Corporation, Bombay.

This exhibition has been made possible only through the generous participation of the filmmakers and producers concerned.